Starting and Ending with Thinking in Social Studies:

Utilizing Historical Thinking Skills in the 21st Century

Theresa Tillotson and Kelsey Toms

Library of Congress Control Number: 2022906219
Tillotson, Theresa. Toms, Kelsey. Starting and Ending with Thinking in Social Studies: Utilizing Historical Thinking Skills in the 21st Century.
    1. Education & Reference > Education > Secondary
    2. Education & Reference > Education > Teaching Methods & Materials > Social Science
        I. Tillotson, Theresa, 1973-
        II. Toms, Kelsey, 1993-

Includes references
ISBN 979-8-9857400-1-1 (pbk.)

Cover design, interior design, and typesetting by Kelsey Toms

At the time of this book's publication, all facts and figures cited are the most current available. If you find an error, please contact T&T Publishing at (210) 802-5855.

T&T Publishing House
San Antonio, TX
(210) 802-5855
tillotsonandtoms@gmail.com

Table of Contents

Reasoning and Research

The Historical Thinking Skills

How to Make it Work

Chapter 1:

Disciplinary Social Studies

When new teachers go through their introduction to pedagogy, there is a significant amount of theory offered. Yet inevitably, the actual classroom experience of their first year is much more difficult than expected and they discover they are less prepared to implement theories with their unique live audiences than they were promised. Likely in succeeding years, that new teacher, if not properly supported, may find themselves facing issues of isolation, discontent, frustration, and even discouragement given all the issues that teachers in the American education system face on a daily basis. Yet the inner voice which convinced that new teacher that education really could be as noble a profession as they originally envisioned keeps them coming back each fall hoping this year will be different. In truth, teaching can be what was promised, so long as the teacher feels as though their efforts are supported, even if they are seeing slow progress in a student's cognitive ability. For student development to happen, teachers need to successfully teach transfer goals through skill focused vertical alignment. The school year will be more effectively utilized and feel more meaningful for teachers and students if students leave the classroom with the ability to think critically and independently about not just academic endeavors, but the world.

Veterans know that "Good teaching is good teaching," that student growth comes from quality teaching, not just from the latest buzzwords the district decides to focus on that year. Experienced teachers know that many good theories and strategies about teaching are recycled, repackaged, and represented as new ideas. Quality teachers know, and research has proven, that making assignments "harder" by offering longer assignments is not the same as increasing rigor. Yet even the most astute teachers may have a niggling feeling that they are missing some key component in their practice because they may not know how best to modify for rigor or how to most effectively present it to the students. Rigor is not "more", rigor is purposeful complexity. Self-awareness and reflection will be of paramount importance to understanding and implementing the work contained in this volume to successfully modify teaching practices. This book will help teachers scaffold rigorous critical thinking skills that will engage more students by meeting them in their abstract thinking proximal zone of development.

Social Studies as a Discipline

Metacognition, or the process of thinking about thinking, must first be practiced by the teacher in order to be conveyed to the students clearly. This is critical to ensuring that students can be trained to think abstractly and on command in the social sciences, and then in their lives. In a "google-able" world, students may benefit from an ability to recall facts, but this act *alone* makes them less useful to society than a search engine which can scour the entire internet for information. A modern teacher, preparing students to launch a career in a world full of technology and computers, must first ask themselves, "How is my role different than that of a search engine?" Once the teacher accepts that their strategy must evolve beyond that of information dissemination, the next critical question to ask is, "What can I teach the students that will make them more useful than a search engine?" To be a productive member of society, new connections and conclusions about information need to be drawn and be made deliverable in order to differentiate man from machine. In the 21st century, teachers MUST make social studies be about more than memorization. Instead, teachers are responsible for employing and educating students in the art of disciplinary historical thinking skills to analyze, evaluate, and synthesize information.

Ease of access to historical sources through databases and search engines has led to the misconception that the value of collected historical works and one's ability to contribute to this particular discipline has decreased. In some ways, ease of access to historical information has created for social studies a reputation that the entire discipline is easy. Even though information can be easily accessed electronically in the 21st century, the discipline itself is just as complex and nuanced as it always has been. If anything, the thinking skills required of the discipline have become even more essential as time passes and the accumulation of human experiences has expanded. The general public accepts that primary sources are as accurate as they are ever going to be because the sources are from the time that is being studied and are therefore more accurate to history than a modern perspective. However, the social studies discipline then requires the ability to think critically and extrapolate from those primary sources in order to think beyond what the biased and incomplete primary source says on the surface. The disciplinary skills allow historians to form hypotheses and run thinking experiments about likely causal factors of the events recorded in the sources, to make effective comparisons between issues and events, to consider context influencing the perspective of the author, and to evaluate continuities and changes over time in the era of the source. The best laboratory that can be offered to students for thought experiments utilizing these critical thinking skills is that of history.

Both children and adults will be quick to say that they hated history in school, despite a natural curiosity with which virtually all children begin learning. This unfortunate outcome is the result of exposure to the field through the narrow lens of teaching the minimum information required in a survey of history, not a study of it. Too often, memorizing dead people's names, learning dates of events, and death by PowerPoint culminate in only superficial multiple choice tests which can kill natural curiosity. It is no wonder then that respect and appreciation for social studies can be lost early in learning. It is not until college or later in life, when people find social studies engaging; when they stumble upon authentic stories and events that capture their imagination and reignite their curiosity without school-imposed structure. In an era of easy access, it is more essential than ever that students leave the classroom with an appreciation of historical thinking skills. Memorized facts that lack significance simply will not be retained, knowing that it can be Googled later anyway. Later in life, with maturity and distance from the focus on memorization, many adults find that they do indeed have a natural appreciation for history.

When the focus is on the thinking and nuance of engaging and relevant topics, adults will find interest in them. They may find themselves reading biographies and watching documentaries voluntarily as these draw conclusions that prove universal and may provide opportunities for reflection and insight into personal issues as well. History taught at the college level is often more engaging for students because it is a model for teaching history well, particularly in upper level courses. While there are lectures, college classes focus on depth of understanding rather than breadth of content covered, which helps encourage mastery and thus confidence, as well as increasing engagement through discussions utilizing historical thinking skills that actively stretch the brain and provide a challenge to be met by students. Elementary and secondary social studies teachers, who want to encourage an appreciation of collective human experience and create lifelong learners must treat it as a discipline like upper division college classes do. This will make students active participants in the stories of history, rather than passive outside observers receiving information.

Structure of this Manual

This book is a manual of thinking paradigms and algorithms in social studies instruction to help students discover new ways to think on command and with intent through historical thinking skills. This system in no way compromises scope and sequence or content coverage. Instead, it leverages the content through employment of analytical thinking by purposefully designing engaging lessons, exercises, and assessments. Teachers can employ the various tools and practices of the social studies discipline using metacognition, task verbs, feedback language, and argumentation to enhance acumen when it comes to actively pursuing thinking in any academic or vocational field. This book provides the student friendly and purposeful systems of thinking that can be used to build clear, communicable transfer goals that are the focus of yearlong instruction.

Each skill chapter will focus on one of seven skills:

- causation (c/e)
- comparison (c/c)
- contextualization (c/x)
- continuity and change over time (CCOT)
- interpretation (I)
- evaluation (E)
- synthesis (S)

The seven skills will be presented in their individual chapters, then a chapter on argumentation will outline application of analytical skills in essay writing.

Each chapter will offer concrete examples of how to break down those skills into formulaic strategies of abstract thinking, provide scaffolding sentence stems and graphic organizers, identify common misconceptions from students and how to fix them, as well as provide specific examples from a variety of social studies subjects. Each subject will use the same content topic as an example across each skill to illustrate the flexible nature of skills based teaching:

Focus on One Skill a Year to Start

"Although we as a team implemented the entire historical thinking skills system in one year, it still took years for us to diagnose and process each of the skills and learn how to integrate them into the content we were already doing in our AP classes. When our school asked us to make a student learning objective for every year as part of our professional development goal, we decided that we would focus on student growth in one skill per year. This allowed us to really focus on the nature of each skill and reflect on what metacognition was happening in a very deliberate way that affected cognitive change. If using all the skills at once is feeling a bit daunting, consider implementing only one or two for the first couple years to become more familiar with the system and gain confidence. Unlike other holistic systems, skills focused teaching takes significant dedication and large quantities of time to implement in its entirety. But focusing on only a few skills for an entire academic year will help to make sure you are using the skills correctly and without overwhelming yourself. It will also allow for internalizing of the skills as each person on the team diagnoses challenges."

– Toms and Tillotson

- Geography utilizes landforms
- World History utilizes World War II
- United States History utilizes the American Revolution
- Government utilizes branches of the federal government
- Economics utilizes supply and demand
- Psychology utilizes learning

It is worthwhile to note that techniques offered in one troubleshooting section to resolve a specific issue can, with adaptation, be leveraged across various skills highlighted in other chapters as well. After each skill chapter is a page dedicated to reflecting on each skill to practice metacognition and take a brain break from admittedly dense concepts. We strongly encourage you to reflect on each skill individually before proceeding through the manual. Also, be sure to watch for vignettes like the one above which narrate the trials of implementation and offer a break from the density of this mindset shift.

As an educator, high expectations regarding critical thinking skills requires clear communication about how to perform abstract thinking. The resources provided in this book, if implemented as outlined, will allow students to more readily grasp and understand the thinking skills so that they are able to apply them intentionally and with confidence. In addition, this system helps students develop a growth mindset and the abstract thinking flexibility that transcends the classroom and enhances employability in the 21st century.

Chapter 2:

Bloom's Taxonomy and Task Verbs

The History of Bloom's Taxonomy

Too often when trying to bring higher levels of thinking to the classroom, teachers with the best intentions decide to offer "more" tasks to increase rigor. However, rigor comes from complexity of thought, not the number of tasks. In this way, students should actually be asked to turn in less "work" but of a more complex nature. Teachers with a repertoire of higher order thinking skills they would like students to exhibit can endlessly create rigorous student-centered activities and assessments. One of the clearest research-based systems to utilize as a language for abstract thinking is Bloom's Taxonomy. First theorized by the educational psychologist Benjamin (B. S.) Bloom in 1956, Bloom's Taxonomy has become a staple in classrooms and education theories. It provides a classification of levels of abstract thinking to utilize as goals for student work, from lowest level of complexity to the highest: (1) knowledge, (2) comprehension, (3) application, (4) analysis, (5) synthesis, and (6) evaluation.

Researchers revised the cognitive process dimensions in Bloom's Taxonomy in 2001, although the updated version retains the same name (Anderson et al., 2001). These new classifications became verbs, rather than nouns, to clarify relationships and add depth of understanding for teachers:

Bloom's Taxonomy as of 2001
(1) remembering (2) understanding (3) applying (4) analyzing (5) evaluating (6) creating

While repackaged and rebranded often in education, Bloom's Taxonomy is the clearest and most common system of language to use when describing abstract thinking. The historical thinking skills proposed in this book fit, and are best understood, within this framework.

Bloom's Taxonomy can be segmented into two parts: "Lower Bloom's" and "Upper Bloom's". This distinction will be referred to in succeeding chapters and therefore, it is worth clarifying at the outset.

Lower Bloom's is the less intensive basic content processing levels:
    (1) remembering,
    (2) understanding, and
    (3) applying.

Upper Bloom's is more intensive higher level abstract thinking:
    (4) analyzing,
    (5) evaluating, and
    (6) synthesizing/creating.

In order to perform Upper Bloom's abstract thinking, students must be able to understand and apply the content. Providing formal instruction to students regarding the different portions of Bloom's will allow students to develop a common academic language and take more ownership of the lower levels of thinking so that the teacher can focus on coaching and scaffolding the Upper Bloom's levels in the classroom. To do so, students need to own their responsibilities in secondary education for the more basic Lower Bloom's levels which generally cannot be scaffolded effectively because of their simplicity.

Lower Bloom's Taxonomy

An anchor chart of Bloom's Taxonomy, and its connection to the historical thinking skills, posted in the classroom can be immensely helpful in maintaining rigor by reminding students of their responsibilities and the higher order thinking skills that are the focus of instruction. The Lower Bloom's skills are shown in the table below:

Lower Bloom's Taxonomy			
	History	*Mathematics*	*Laundry*
(1) Remembering	The Declaration of Independence was published in 1776.	2 + 2 = 4	Washing clothes requires special soap.
(2) Understanding	The Declaration of Independence told England America wanted to be a separate country from them.	"+" symbol means to add	Once clothes are washed, they will need to be dried before they can be worn.
(3) Applying	The ideas of equality in the Declaration of Independence were also used to inspire the French Revolution.	"+" symbol means to add, and this can be used with different variables 3 + 5 = ?	While all clothes need soap and water, whites can safely be bleached

The lowest level of thinking is (1) remembering, which is a basic recall of facts. No true understanding of the information is required, as often remembering manifests itself as lists of information, which in a history class usually means copying from notes or a textbook. The next level up in Lower Bloom's is (2) understanding, which is where a student can take the information they memorized and describe it in their own words. No abstract thinking is required when describing a connection that has already been made by the teacher for the students. The top level of Lower Bloom's is (3) applying. Applying requires students to utilize information that was previously remembered and understood by the students in a new context, but is often teacher directed and still ends up being a summary of content. As the teacher is supplying the application context, the practice ends up being a superficial approximation of more rigor in the classroom.

True application should be student generated, because applying is simply the launch pad for higher level abstract thinking. While application is necessary to analysis, teachers should not settle for assessing such a foundational skill because it will give students a false sense of competency in critical thinking. Teachers should instead push students to more advanced thinking levels before assessment is conducted. Thus, in a more rigorous course, application will be inherently required to perform well on assessment tasks.

Lower Bloom's thinking is associated with rudimentary processes that students in elementary education are exposed to and in which eventually become superficially proficient. In order to continue to develop students, the secondary education teacher should then simply offer techniques to remember, understand, and apply along with an expectation that the students are responsible for those skills. For example, in the secondary level the teacher can provide tutoring, offer reminders about basic study skills, mnemonic devices for memorization, refreshers on research skills, offer organizational acronyms, and create lessons that curate basic information for students to then employ.

Note, that the suggestions above require the students to become active participants in their education. Despite providing relevant, engaging, and best practice lessons, teachers cannot memorize or understand *for students*. Teachers cannot control how students spend their time outside of the classroom, nor can they generate intrinsic motivation for students. For these reasons, it is imperative that the teacher establish from the outset of the year, that basic understanding of content is the student's responsibility in secondary education. This allows the teacher to spend their valuable time offering feedback and lessons that scaffold Upper Bloom's abstract thinking.

Upper Bloom's Taxonomy

"Upper Bloom's" Taxonomy			
	History	*Mathematics*	*Laundry*
(4) Analyzing	Thomas Jefferson was inspired by Enlightenment philosophers like John Locke, so the Declaration of Independence is a reflection of Enlightenment ideology.	Breaking down and explaining reasons for why these two equations arrive at the same answer: $2 + 2 = 4$ $2 \times 2 = 4$	If bleach is to be used, it will be more effective with hot water than with cold water.
(5) Evaluating	The Declaration of Independence was more of an appeal to Parliament regarding grievances than a declaration of war.	Diagnosing which operations need to be completed and in what order to arrive at the correct response.	The temperature of the water should be selected based on the fabric being laundered.
(6) Synthesizing /Creating	Painting an abstraction of themes and feelings expressed in the Declaration of Independence with a paragraph that explains each symbolic choice.	Generating an original word problem using the principles being studied.	A washing machine can be used to dye material too, resulting in a completely new use for, and product from, a laundry cycle.

Educators need to require more than summaries as evidence of mastery, and instead expect the students to produce documentation of independent thought they created themselves as outlined in the three levels of Upper Bloom's: (4) analyzing, (5) evaluating, and (6) creating/synthesizing.

(4) **Analyzing** is deconstructing a topic into parts in order to diagnose and build new meaningful connections between the parts.

(5) **Evaluating** is weighing evidence and choosing an argument.

(6) **Synthesizing** (Creating) is generating new ideas and new connections between two seemingly disparate topics.

This work will provide instruction in how to scaffold historical thinking skills at these top three levels to provide rigor and metacognitively teach abstract thinking.

It is important to note that while the 2001 revision of Bloom's taxonomy changed the language of one thinking level from synthesis to creating, this work will retain the use of synthesis for its definitional clarity in the thinking process. In educational circles, "creating" has sometimes been diluted to the production of an alternative medium of submission that only employs Lower Bloom's skills. For example, inaccurately termed performance assessments might take the form of posters, pamphlets, PowerPoints, or art pieces that, despite being aesthetically pleasing, only require the students to list information about a topic, categorize terms, describe definitions in their own words, or include pictures relevant to the topic at hand rather than actually synthesize. These attempts at "creating" do not provide evidence of critical thinking, so the use of the word "synthesis" in setting expectations for performance assessments encourages the employment of abstract thinking that requires the genuine *creation of connections* between topics.

Challenging students to high levels of thinking increases interest, engagement, student participation, and can ultimately lead to higher levels of intrinsic motivation through habitual perseverance even if increased rigor is resisted at first. Education researcher Robert Marzano (2019b, p. 1) describes the cognitive analysis aspect of rigor as "discerning new relationships between topics and new distinctions within topics." Here, one could argue, Marzano identifies analysis, evaluation, and synthesis, as defined in this work, as necessary for rigor. Marzano (2019b, p. 2) also holds that creating rigor through a focus on asking higher-order questioning is too simple and does not significantly affect learning outcomes. *However, this book does not argue that teachers should just ask complex questions, but instead offers techniques for teachers to ask cognitively complex questions and to educate students in the metacognition and abstract thinking skills necessary to answer such questions.*

Cognitive scientists tend to differentiate between declarative and procedural knowledge acquisition (Marzano, 2019b). Declarative knowledge is informational such as basic data or facts and procedural knowledge is the ability to perform skills and processes. While students do need to learn declarative knowledge about what happened in history, this work argues that a singular focus on teaching information for information's sake is incomplete instruction. The students must learn the procedural knowledge of historical thinking skills as the focus of the discipline to be used in conjunction with an understanding of historical issues, events, and ideas. True evidence of mastery requires both of these types of knowledge to be on display: the understanding (declarative) and skillful analysis (procedural) of information. For this reason, the historical thinking skills outlined in this book fall only in Upper Bloom's. Causation, comparison, contextualization, change and continuity over time, and interpretation are *systems of analysis*. These skills accompanied by evaluation and synthesis, generate opportunities to practice the procedural knowledge necessary in a more rigorous practice of the social studies discipline that elevates simple declarative instruction.

Intentional Instruction of Academic Task Verbs

Although teachers are familiar with the verbs associated with Bloom's Taxonomy and may even teach them as part of differentiating higher order thinking skills, *task verbs* need to be taught as an isolated concept as well. Task verbs refer to the product requested from thinking. If students do not have intentional instruction in expectations of output, that is the level of delivery the question calls for, they may be too superficial in their execution of their response. For example, if a question asks students to explain and yet their response offers a simple description, they are not completing the level of recording of their thinking that was required. To remedy this, task verbs should be highlighted through intentional instruction. Separating out the thinking regarding the content and the expectation for successful delivery of an answer will lead to more student success.

Using a consistent metaphor throughout the initial explanation of academic task verbs will allow students to compare and see differences between what each verb is asking a student to record. "Tying a shoe" is used in the anchor handouts in the next two pages and a second analogy can be explained verbally to the whole class such as baking a cake, learning to drive, or any other multi-step task. A myriad of examples, particularly those utilizing prior knowledge, show students that the verbs can be applied in multiple authentic contexts. Printable versions of the "Common Task Verbs" handouts are available in the Reproducibles section at the end of the book.

Lower Blooms Common Task Verbs

Different skills require different tasks. Questions may call for <u>more than one task</u>, such as both to identify and explain. Some tasks are more complex than others. For example, composing a list may only require a complete sentence, but one may need to write several paragraphs for a satisfactory discussion, including well-developed examples as support, in order to adequately explain some phenomenon.

List/Identify: Listing or identifying is a task that requires no more than a <u>simple enumeration</u> of some factors or characteristics. A list <u>does not require any</u> causal <u>explanations</u>.
- ***To Tie a Shoe**: Items required include shoes, holes in the shoe for laces, and shoelaces*
- ***In History Class**: You might be asked to list or identify three characteristics Presidents consider when making appointments, so one might include party, race, gender, etc.*

Define: A definition requires you to <u>provide a meaning</u> for a word or concept. <u>Examples may help</u> to demonstrate understanding of the definition.
- ***To Tie a Shoe**: Is to tighten a shoe around one's foot so the shoe is not easily removed.*
- ***In History Class**: You may be instructed to write what the Presidential cabinet is in your own words.*

Describe: A description involves providing a <u>depiction or portrayal</u> of a phenomenon or its most significant characteristics. Descriptions most often address "what" questions.
- ***To Tie a Shoe**: Pulling together and securing of the laces with a tie or bow as a closure.*
- ***In History Class**: You may be asked to describe reasons for the decline in voter turnout, in the description you must do <u>more than simply list facts</u>—you must actually describe the reasons. For example, you may describe that the expansion of suffrage <u>led to</u> a decline in overall voter turnout because once voting was made available to more individuals, the overall percentage of those voting declined.*

Discuss: Discussions generally require that you <u>explore relationships</u> between different concepts or phenomena. Identifying, describing, and explaining could be required tasks involved in writing a satisfactory discussion.
- ***To Tie a Shoe**: Not all shoes lace; shoes not "required" to stay on might not have them.*
- ***In History Class**: Do application level thinking, for example, a discussion prompt might require you to differentiate between demographic characteristics and how they align with the two primary political ideologies.*

Upper Blooms Common Task Verbs

Explain: An explanation involves the exploration of <u>possible causal relationships</u>. When providing explanations, you should identify and discuss <u>logical connections or causal patterns</u> that exist between or among various phenomena.

- *To Tie a Shoe: Take one lace in each hand, cross laces, and tuck lace A under lace B...*
- *In History Class: You need to record the critical thinking that you performed in a coherent way.*

Analyze: This task usually requires <u>separating</u> a phenomenon into its component parts or characteristics as a <u>way of understanding the whole</u>. An analysis should yield explicit conclusions that are explained or supported by specific evidence and/or well-reasoned arguments.

- *To Tie a Shoe: A child will be less proficient at tying shoes than an adult due to 1) a lack of coordination in fine motor skills, 2) fewer years of practice and experience, 3) a lack of motivation as a result of inexperience with causes/effects of tripping and injury.*
- *In History Class: Do the causation, comparison, contextualization, interpretation, and/or change and continuity over time skill.*

Compare/Contrast: This task requires you to make specific links between two or more concepts or phenomena. You should understand that it is important to note <u>similarities AND differences</u> between the concepts or phenomena under consideration.

- *To Tie a Shoe: Wet shoelaces might be harder to untie than dry shoelaces.*
- *In History Class: Do the comparison skill.*

Evaluate/Assess: An evaluation or assessment involves considering <u>how well something meets a certain standard</u>, and as such, generally requires a thesis. It is important to identify the criteria used in the evaluation. If no criteria are explicitly given in the question, you should take care to clearly identify the ones that you choose to employ. Specific examples may be applied to the criteria to support your thesis. Evaluation or assessment requires explicit connections between the thesis or argument and the supporting evidence.

- *To Tie a Shoe: Shoes with laces are MORE appropriate for gym classes than shoes without laces i.e., 1) tend to come with better grip on the outer sole, 2) better safety/security at higher speeds and levels of activity, 3) enhanced confidence leading to better performance in athletic events*
- *In History Class: Answer an evaluation prompt or answer a "To what extent" prompt.*

Transfer Goals as the Focus of Backwards Planning

As discussed in the first chapter, modern teachers must ask: "What can I teach the students that will make them more useful than a search engine?" Indeed, the 21st century teacher must focus on which transfer goals the students need to develop in order to provide flexible skills to adapt to tomorrow's workplace and new technologies. Wiggins and McTighe, authors of the *Understanding by Design* curriculum, identify the ultimate aim of education to be a student's ability to take a skill and use it autonomously in a new context (2011, p. 14). The type of learning target for this level of application is a transfer goal. For example, one such transfer goal could be utilizing math learned in school to complete taxes. Therefore, Wiggins and McTighe argue, teachers must utilize backwards planning by identifying transfer goals and then intentionally scaffolding practice of the identified skill goals starting from day one through the end of the year (2011, p. 7). When goals are purposeful and focused, students, parents, and teachers all have a clear direction for supporting the student's progress and goals. Learning to leverage the valuable academic vocabulary of this chapter will allow students to reflect on and build critical thinking skills in an effort to reach their goals. Focusing on transferability of skills in the social studies classroom enables teachers to be able to readily highlight the value of class activities and provide for authenticity of instruction by encouraging student engagement and reflective practices like metacognition. By mastering these thinking skills in the social studies classroom, students can then adapt each of them to their adult lives, enabling learning to transcend the classroom and empowering them to thrive in the ever-changing 21st century.

Chapter 3:

Metacognition and Narrative Feedback

The Necessity of Metacognition

Metacognition is likely the most underrated skill a quality teacher needs to employ. The reason for this is that it does not come naturally and is not often overtly emphasized in teacher preparation courses. It requires not only practicing self-awareness, but then reflecting upon what has been discovered when it comes to the thinking process. For teachers to be able to effectively teach thinking skills, they must understand what is happening in their own brains as thinking occurs. Only then will they be able to effectively assess what is happening in their students' thinking processes and communicate such complex metacognition to their students. In this way students too can become both self-aware and reflective about thinking.

For example, when children learn how to bake or to grill from a mother or father who has this skill, the child's skill level will often reflect that of the parent if direct instruction has taken place. But fathers who are good bakers learn from mistakes because they reflect on what went well with the recipe, how the cooking time and temperature affected the final outcome, and compare the results to previous attempts. This too then is communicated to the child who is learning how to bake. All of these reflective practices allow for more predictable and successful products in future attempts for both the father and the child. Likewise, metacognition is required of the teacher both in school and out of it, in order to model for and instruct students in this critical practice when development in skills is the objective.

In order for the teacher to master the techniques of self-reflection and increase self-awareness they must be able to communicate to students the steps associated with critical thinking. This allows for a student to be able to employ those steps to determine where their thinking needs improvement and where their strengths lie so as to replicate successful thinking patterns. In essence, teachers must become proficient at reflecting on and performing historical thinking skills themselves if they are to be successful at introducing students to the skills of metacognition and abstract historical thinking. Education researcher John Hattie (2012) found in his meta-analysis that "teacher clarity" had a exceedingly high effect size of .75 toward desired student outcomes. Clarity then, as a goal, becomes one of the most important focal points a teacher should attend to in their classroom. In order to offer clarity to the students, the teacher must have a thorough understanding of both the skills and how to articulate them. This can only be achieved through meaningful metacognition.

Employing metacognition is necessary to achieve mastery, be it the teacher's mastery of instruction or the student's mastery of historical thinking skills. Marzano and Toth (2013) explain common behaviors exhibited by people trying to become an expert in any field, including breaking down necessary skills, focusing on critical skill chunks in practice, receiving quality feedback from experienced coaches, and continuing to practice identified skills at increasingly challenging levels. These behaviors that lead to becoming an expert may occur by default or without reflection but employing these metacognitive skills with intent will help students learn how to develop mastery in a more efficient and productive way.

Modeling Metacognition

"I found that as I enhanced my own metacognition practices, my students could benefit from my experience through narrative modeling of what my thought process was. This began in tutoring sessions where I would talk out the literal thoughts I was having when I provided feedback on an assigned skill task. I would read what they wrote aloud, then elaborate on the narrative feedback helping make the connections of reflection for the student. After I saw the benefits for the students in tutoring, I started incorporating metacognitive narration into even my lectures for whole class instruction. As I increased my own awareness of my internal dialogue, I realized that articulating my thought process created a classroom culture of metacognition. While it does require some vulnerability, this was one of the most effective ways to incorporate skills instruction into my everyday classroom, including something as traditional as lecture style teaching practices."

– Tillotson

Teachers too, will become increasingly proficient in their craft and will be able to model metacognitive behaviors for their students. Through repeated attempts and consistent quality feedback on specific skills, coupled with self-reflection, students can and will grow their capacity to think critically.

Growth Mindset

Often students have been trained throughout their academic career to focus on grades as the end goal. However, this can sabotage their progress toward the more skill focused transfer goals. Therefore, a shift needs to be made to a learning-oriented focus or a growth mindset. This theory was outlined by American psychologist Carol Dweck in her 2006 book *Mindset: The New Psychology of Success*. Dweck (2006) argues that a growth mindset is one where people believe that their qualities and abilities can grow and change from personal efforts aimed at improvement. If a person maintains a growth mindset that person is more likely to embrace challenges, develop grit to overcome failure, see hard work as the key to mastery, learn from criticism, and find inspiration in the success of others. With these habits, people with growth mindsets consistently see higher levels of achievement. Thus, the growth mindset is essential to the classroom.

If students can be introduced to the significance of small steps within their zone of proximal development, they will learn to systematically challenge themselves in appropriate ways. This will allow them to become more comfortable with working outside of their comfort zone, a requirement for growth and learning. Once students become appreciative of the process of learning, as opposed to solely focusing on the end result, they will be more willing to abandon their grade-oriented perspective and adopt a growth mindset.

The learning-oriented growth mindset is a necessity in a skill focused classroom because progress is incremental and often not as tangible as a grade-oriented focus. In fact,

> ### Building Vulnerability
>
> "While we all know that students take some time to warm up to a new teacher each academic year, it takes even longer for a student who is in the first year in a skills-based classroom to acclimate to a growth mindset. My students typically come to me primed to receive "good grades" for simple compliance. Receiving their first low marks almost always has them backpedaling and withdrawing. My students were afraid of embarrassment and thought unsuccessful practice was equal to failure. I decided to model vulnerability myself, so I actively questioned my own thinking in class discussions and overtly admitted and apologized to the whole class for mistakes I made. By modeling a growth mindset, I not only gained respect, but also generated risk-taking behavior in students who saw me take chances, fail, and survive to get better over time. Acknowledging imperfection in public is a challenge for teachers trained to be unquestionable authority figures in their classrooms. Yet when I modeled self-acceptance, and created clear expectations for errors, my students would allow themselves to be vulnerable enough to grow in their skills. Because of the cognitive intimacy that develops in a safe learning environment, I got to know my students in a much deeper way and felt more rewarded with my chosen profession than I ever had before. It allowed me to build not just skills, but to influence personality and ideological developments that encouraged students to calculate and take educated risks."
>
> – Tillotson

depending on how much exposure students have had to practicing critical thinking, some will find themselves "failing" at these historical thinking skills more often than not, particularly in the beginning of the year. The teacher must make sure that all students, particularly the ones who are used to regularly receiving high marks, understand that they are not expected to be proficient at abstract thinking at the beginning of the year, but must put every effort into practicing toward that goal even when only small changes will be shown over time. Students must be taught that multiple unsuccessful attempts and additional practice are not the equivalent of failure but are critical to success. Through a focus on developing a growth mindset and the practice of perseverance, students can learn to appreciate the minor advancements they are making toward the transfer goals that culminate in measurable growth over time.

The Necessity of Giving and Teaching Narrative Feedback

Providing narrative feedback to students that utilizes the language of Bloom's taxonomy and task verbs is critical for the growth process to take place and instrumental in developing a growth mindset when it comes to skill development. In *Formative Assessment and Standards-Based Grading*, Marzano (2010) outlines the most significant findings done by researchers regarding feedback. One study by Kluger and DeNisi in 1996 found that feedback that does not tell students how they can improve actually decreases student achievement. A 2007 synthesis of meta-analyses by Hattie and Timperley found, essentially, just telling students they are doing a "good job" will not improve outcomes; students need specific feedback that tells them how to improve their performance. Another study by Stuart Yeh in 2008 showed that students who received feedback did more work, and more accurate work, than those students who did not get feedback. When the feedback was no longer given to those students the accuracy and completion rate fell. Indeed, John Hattie (2012) also emphasizes the importance of feedback in learning outcomes in his later *Visible Learning* publications, as he found feedback to have a remarkably high effect size of .70 toward desired student outcomes. Without overt instruction, students cannot effectively tell themselves how to get better. This then is the teacher's role in the classroom: to share the burden of reflecting on progress. Therefore, quality narrative feedback that specifically tells students what they need to do to improve their performance is critical to the success of the students.

Research shows that student performance cannot be enhanced by letter grades or numbers alone, much less abstract thinking. To this end, when teaching critical thinking, there is a significant need for narrative feedback to be offered in order to facilitate reflection and concrete application of the feedback. For the overburdened teacher, which is most of them, this can be a daunting requirement in trying to increase the rigor of a classroom, but it does not have to be. One of the most effective ways to increase student independence in reflection on their thinking is to also introduce a common language for feedback so that students can effectively implement changes to their work. It is quite common for teachers to overestimate how much feedback language their students actually understand. If the student has underdeveloped writing skills, they may not know what teacher feedback means, much less how to improve their work. Therefore, communicating with students a feedback language which tells them what they should actually do with teacher feedback is critical.

Intentional Instruction of Academic Feedback Language

Teaching academic feedback language should begin the first time student work is returned. If common academic language in feedback is introduced in formal lessons and becomes a part of the learning, students will be able to more readily interpret the skill focused language as well. Student understanding of feedback language will help them not only to interpret professor's feedback in college, but also feedback in the workplace as an adult, another transfer goal. When students regularly use the same academic language as the teacher, feedback can be streamlined and even abbreviated yet it retains its value. The way to accomplish the development of independence in metacognition is to teach the students the meaning of academic feedback language and academic verbs consistently and thoroughly throughout the year.

To begin teaching the students the metacognition of considering feedback is best introduced to the whole class in order to establish the expectation of rigor, and then consistently throughout the year in warm-ups or other activities. When feedback is given for the first time, take the opportunity to introduce common academic feedback language and teach students what it means, referring to an anchor chart and a handout with an outline of common feedback. Then, further refining can take place during in class activities and tutoring.

On the next page is a sample anchor chart of feedback language. It is recommended that either this, or a similar anchor chart developed by the teacher is posted in the classroom as well as providing printed copies for the students. However, it is important to personalize the feedback language to what comes naturally to each teacher so that it is authentic and teachers are more likely to stay consistent in the language they use. A printable version of the "What does my feedback mean?" one-pager is available in the Reproducibles section at the end of the book.

What does my feedback mean?

Vague/Example? - You need to add specific examples and evidence.
Vague: America is free.
Specific/Not vague: America ensures inalienable rights **such as** life, liberty, and the pursuit of happiness.

Connect ideas- You need to put the two ideas together in one sentence to argue a point.
Not connected: America is dramatic in elections. There was one in 2016.
Connected: America is dramatic in elections, **as seen in** the presidential election of 2016.

Does not support argument- You need better evidence to support your response to the prompt *or* change your argument.
Does not support argument: America is awesome because we fight lots of wars.
Supports argument: America is awesome because there is free K-12 education.
OR America sometimes makes bad choices by fighting too many wars.

Does not answer/argue/reference prompt- The evidence you provided is not on the topic of the prompt. You are missing the connection to the prompt.
Does not respond to prompt:
Prompt: Has America's economy crashed?
Answer: The Cold War was against the USSR. (evidence is off theme and topic and it doesn't mention economy)
Responds to prompt: Answer: America's economy crashed in the Great Depression.

So what?/Finish your thought - Why is this important? What is the significance? Why does the idea matter? How does it connect to the prompt?
Lacks the "so what": America is a representative democracy.
Has the "so what": America is a representative democracy, **so** the government is designed to reflect what the people want through representation and voting.

Incomplete sentence- You are either missing the subject or object of your sentence so it doesn't make sense or answer the prompt completely.
Incomplete Sentence: Because it helps the economy. (What does?? IDK!)
Complete Sentence: America builds infrastructure **because** it helps the economy.

Confusing - I could not understand your grammar or reasoning. Start over.

Not quite/not really- Response is very problematic and probably historically inaccurate. Start over.

When the academic feedback verbs are taught to the whole class, the teacher can expound upon challenges seen by a large number of students so that further instruction, remediation, and clarification of thinking skills can occur in a large group setting. It is critical to distinguish between content misconceptions and inaccurate critical thinking. Content misconceptions may be addressed in future classes, but the focus of a debrief of an assigned critical thinking task should be to highlight opportunities for students to practice metacognition with feedback language as well as historical skill development. When offering feedback, it often helps in one-on-one settings to meet with students individually to have them observe as the teacher models evaluation of submitted work. If teachers are willing to orate while they are practicing critical thinking in front of a student, the student can benefit from observing an auditory reflection of the teacher's internal dialogue and is more likely to see successful replication of this technique for himself. While editorially sharing the internal dialogue with a sample essay for the whole class is a technique that can be employed in large group settings, it is even more effective to work

> ### Digging the Moat
> "A couple of years after implementing the historical thinking skills with my AP US History students I decided to diversify by teaching Pre-AP World Geography so that I could try to scaffold down the skills and vertically align our honors history program. With the freshmen in Geography, I found myself working with students fresh out of middle school whose abstract thinking had only just developed and who were not proficient in persuasive writing. I decided to slowly integrate the skills one by one but found myself with too little time to teach everything I wanted to without overwhelming them. I had the students practice analyzing documents and writing introductory paragraphs; however, they were just barely scratching the surface of understanding the skills. I knew, because of the compounding nature of skills, that it was better to teach only a few skills well, than all of them poorly. After lamenting to her how ineffective I felt, Tillotson gave me a metaphor that bolstered my hope: 'When the kids leave high school, they will be a fully built castle. In freshman year you are only digging the moat, no one expects walls to be built! Their sophomore year they will get a foundation, junior year walls, and by senior year maybe a roof. They probably won't get pretty turrets and flags until well into college. Dig the moat as best you can and teach them what they can handle so that they will be ready for their castle foundation next year.' Relieved, I was reminded how important like-minded educators are to the process of implementing metacognition and skills. Moral support is invaluable."
>
> – Toms

with a student one-on-one using his or her essay to divulge particular points of confusion for that student and clarify troubleshooting techniques.

Particularly with middle or early high school students, consistent implementation of feedback instruction is important for students to internalize the language of academia. One idea for consistent implementation of instruction is through teaching writing in warmups by focusing on one element of feedback that might be typically offered on submitted assignments utilizing content recently taught. The employment and debrief of warmups help students differentiate between diverse types of feedback. The debrief will likely include good and bad examples as well as an opportunity for students to actively practice fixing their writing. Through practicing with feedback in a warmup activity, students can learn how to make these changes on future submissions independently. These warmups are most successful when used after the language has already been introduced to then reteach or refine the skill of interpreting feedback.

First, remind the class of what the feedback means. For example, using a warmup about vagueness, remind the students that they need to add more details and specificity in terms of the question asked. Then, provide the students an opportunity to utilize notes or even neighbors while they alter the bad example that is provided and make it more successful. As students share how they fixed the work in the debrief, the teacher creates an opportunity to discuss content misconceptions, formatting of historical thinking skills, and most importantly for this activity, how to fix work based on feedback given. These warmups provide formative assessment opportunities for academic feedback language acquisition as well. Examples of warm up prompts are provided in the chart below:

Content Specific Examples of Feedback Language Warmups	
Geography **Make this answer less VAGUE!** *Prompt:* Why is the Amazon Rainforest so important to the world? *Answer:* The Rainforest is important to the world because of air.	**US History** **Please CONNECT THESE IDEAS together!** The Stamp Act Crisis increased tension between the American Colonies and the British Parliament. The Patriots disliked virtual representation.
World History **This DOES NOT ANSWER THE PROMPT, fix!** *Prompt:* Why did the Ottoman Empire collapse? *Answer:* The Ottoman Empire was on the Central Powers side in WWI.	**Government** **Please explain the "SO WHAT?" to this sentence!** The President has powers enumerated in the Constitution.

Creating a New Paradigm

The topics covered in the previous chapter on Bloom's Taxonomy and Task Verbs coupled with the methodology described here, Metacognition and Feedback Language, work together to create a critical thinking focused classroom that allows 21st century students to be competitive in their ability to solve the problems of tomorrow. Through the practice of metacognition, using a common academic language and quality teacher feedback, the classroom will transition to become one focused on a growth mindset and abstract thinking. While this is a more challenging way of approaching contemporary education, it is also more engaging and fulfilling for both teachers and students *once it becomes routine*. The challenge, as with any new paradigm, is to practice perseverance as the classroom shifts to a more skills focused model, leveraging the tenacity to make it through the necessary trial and error process, and encouraging increased stamina for all participants. As will be addressed in the later chapters, this model works best when applied in multiple grade levels to support continuity where vertical alignment is possible. The next several chapters will delve into each individual skill providing meaningful analysis of and practical application tools for how the skills are to be taught and learned.

Chapter 4:

Causation (c/e)

Skill Overview
     Causation is one of the most fundamental skills and arguably the most important as it is a building block for many other skills. It involves analyzing the relationship between causes and effects, most notably, "how" the cause leads to the effect. The "how" should be a narration of connections that walk the reader through the relationship. The formula for causation is "Cause → How → Effect" which can be applied to any prompt or situation when analysis of causal relationships must take place. First, the student must figure out if the topics given in a prompt are the cause, the how, or the effect. Then they must fill in the rest of the formula and write their answer in complete sentences in a conclusion.

How To
     Step 1: Figure out which part of the formula the prompt offers
     Step 2: Fill in the rest of the formula
     Step 3: Organize into a 1-2 sentence conclusion

Graphic Organizer

Cause	How	Effect
Conclusion		

Sentence Stems
     (cause) so (how). Therefore (effect).
     - OR -
     (effect) because (cause) which (how).

Example
When making a cake, the ingredients would be the cause of the cake being made and the finished product would be the effect. However, enacted recipe instructions are the process that explains *how* the cake came to be. The temperature at which it was baked and the length of time in the oven are an integral part of the *process* to explain nuances of the finished product.

Introduction to Causation

The cause and effect skill is often assumed to be mastered by students based on their previous classroom experience, but they usually only have a cursory understanding of the skill. One could argue it may be the first skill infants experience through experimentation. For example, when an infant seated in a highchair throws her toy on the floor and a caregiver picks it up to keep the child from crying, the infant begins to understand that she can have an impact on her environment; that is, she can cause things to happen. Thus, to confirm the result, the infant throws the toy on the floor again, and the caregiver returns the toy to the tray, confirming for the infant that throwing the toy will cause the caregiver to pick it up. Yet, when an older child is asked directly about cause and effect, there is confusion about what causal relationships exist and how they are defined based on a common misunderstanding that the skill only has the two elements of cause and effect. For example, if one were to ask an older sibling what transpired in the previous example he might say, "My baby brother threw a toy, so Mom picked it up" without considering the reason she did so. This superficial observation overlooks the reason *why* Mom picked up the toy: to keep the child from crying. The critical relationship between the cause and effect means that causation is actually a much more nuanced analytical skill that incorporates not just the causal factors and the outcome, but includes the process which explains the connection between them.

How the Skill Works

Thus, the task for the educator is to teach the metacognition that will allow students to recognize the three step thinking pattern of causation so they can perform the thinking skill consciously. As masters of content, teachers focus on conveying causal relationships in historical terms. Yet, by focusing instead on critical thinking and using the content to illustrate how the skill works, classroom activities and discussions will more readily engage critical thinking. Students often have a limited view of causation wherein they believe it only requires memorization of a disconnected list of facts. If causation is not properly investigated, students will not only be limited by the superficial understandings they hold about the content, but will also lack the ability to apply the skill in a novel context and answer more complex questions. Traditionally, when students are presented with "cause and effect" it is shown to them in a graphic organizer containing two boxes labeled "cause" and "effect" with an arrow between them. However, that would never sufficiently answer a causation question if required to do so in the adult world. For example: "Why were you late to work today?"

Cause Coffee	→	Effect Late

This would translate to "I was late to work because of coffee." To most that would be entirely insufficient and leave one wondering what they were expected to understand about the coffee. Observers can now begin to feel what is missing. It is the series of events that transpire between the "cause" and the "effect." Yet even this graphic organizer shows that there is a relationship between the two boxes that too often goes undetected. This relationship is represented by an oversimplified *arrow* which is rarely required to be explained but should actually have its own box. To teach causation, the student needs to investigate the arrow. In student friendly language, this is the "process" or "how it happened".

In order to prevent future misconceptions, students must be taught that there are actually *three* parts to a causal relationship: the cause, "the how", and the effect. Thus, the answer should sound something like: "I was late because I spilled coffee on my shirt and had to take the time to change it, causing me to be late to work." The process through which the coffee caused lateness is the "how". Here, then, is the formula for causation:

Cause	How (→)	Effect
Coffee	Change Clothes	Late

Teaching the Students

Causation is most effectively introduced to the students through real life examples that provide relevance. It is best to begin with simplified analogies, such as the coffee example previously discussed, and intentionally teaching the skill on a designated skill day. Students can then be guided to extrapolate and apply the skill to something more authentic that has happened in their own lives to apply the learning meaningfully, a technique recommended for introducing all the skills. Students can then move into using this new skill in the lab of the social sciences which is less familiar to them. It is also important to note that repetition of the three elements of causation is critical to ensure the students are using this skill like a formula as they would in a science or math class. For the first few prompts of the year, causation can be used to establish that students are expected to memorize formulas. This sets the precedent that other skills may also be learned like a formula as well. For long term modeling, students find an anchor chart on the wall of the classroom to be incredibly helpful. For each skill, the appropriate anchor chart will be provided in their respective chapters, like the one on the next page for causation. Printable versions of all the skill anchor charts are available in the Reproducibles section at the end of the book.

Causation (c/e)

Student can discern whether causes or effects are being assessed in a prompt and accurately respond, isolating causes from and connecting causes to processes and effects.

Cause(s)	How the events happened	Effect(s)

Example:

The apple tree grew because the farmer took the seeds and buried them in the soil in 2008 where they **received the necessary nutrients**.

- OR -

The farmer took the seeds and buried them in the soil in 2008 where they **received the necessary nutrients** so the tree grew.

Although skills are first introduced with non-content examples to create relevancy, the sooner the students can apply the content with the skill, the more effective their retention of the information. In this way, content is not compromised by employing a skills-based approach. Causation, like the other historical thinking skills, must be taught through strategic planning for optimal clarity. It is important to determine what students will be responsible for in answering a prompt on a formal or informal assessment, specifically which part of the causal relationship is being addressed.

The Columbian Exchange, since it is used commonly in social studies, can highlight how application of a skills-based approach works in the reality of the classroom. In analyzing the topic of the Columbian Exchange, students may attempt to focus on extraneous details, misinterpret what a question asks them to highlight and diagnose, and may struggle with the semantics of the English language or their confidence level. It is important to note that student misunderstandings are a key component in skill development as the students reflect on their areas of growth and strategize remedies. The teacher's role then becomes one of strategic scaffolding and individualized diagnostic work which will lead to enhanced student proficiency in the skills over time. Explanations and solutions regarding common student mistakes can be found in the "Troubleshooting" segment of each chapter after the skill is outlined.

It is the teacher's responsibility to determine what content is relevant to answer the prompt by applying the formula so that correct answers can be assessed and troubleshooting of incorrect answers can be conducted. The following boxed formula is an easy scaffolding tool to help students interpret prompts. Students need to be taught to start looking for what part of the formula the prompt provided, because that will inform them specifically what needs to be identified in order to properly respond to the prompt. For example:

<u>"What was ONE effect of the Columbian Exchange?"</u>

Since the cause was supplied by the prompt i.e. the Columbian Exchange, the student needs to supply the how and the effect to sufficiently argue a relevant response.

Cause	How (→)	Effect
The Columbian Exchange	Student needs to list events	Student needs to identify as their main argument
Student Response: *The Columbian Exchange* (cause) *led to increased global biodiversity* (effect) *because of an increase in new trade between the Old and New Worlds* (how).		

<u>"What caused the dramatic drop in Native American populations in the 16th century?"</u>

In this example, the cause and the how have been identified as the content to be argued by the student, whereas the effect has been provided i.e. the drop in Native American populations in the 16th century.

Cause	How (→)	Effect
Student needs to identify as their main argument	Student needs to list events	Drop in Native population
Student Response: *The dramatic drop in Native American population in the 16th century* (effect) *was a result of the Spaniards unknowingly introducing smallpox to the Americas* (cause) *which killed the Natives in record numbers because they had virtually no immunity to the disease* (how).		

<u>"What were the economic causes and effects of the Columbian Exchange?"</u>

At elevated levels, like those in Advanced Placement classes, prompts may provide only the "how" and ask the student to use their context skill to determine both the cause and the effect. In this example, the student must know enough about the Columbian Exchange to create a cause and effect relationship in one cohesive themed argument, in this case economics.

Cause	How (→)	Effect
Student needs to identify, and it must be about the economy	Columbian Exchange	Student needs to identify, and it must be about the economy
Student Response: *The Europeans were trying to make money and collect gold and silver* (cause) *so they started trading with the New World in the Columbian Exchange* (how) *which did help make the Europeans a lot of money by shifting their economies from feudalism to mercantilism* (effect).		

Troubleshooting

Just as it is the teacher's responsibility to understand the content, and assess correct answers, it is also the teacher's responsibility to anticipate where students will struggle. Having names for the types of struggles students face and categorizing examples that teachers see on a regular basis will make feedback more efficient and effective. The teacher then can repetitively clarify misconceptions and consistently provide academic language for students to continue working towards mastery of the skill.

Student Misconception 1: Focusing on extraneous details

In the Columbian Exchange example from earlier in the chapter, the student will first try to remember everything they know about the historical time period. They may generate specific lists of foods exchanged, the number of natives that died due to exposure to new diseases, and the names of Christopher Columbus' three ships. These distractors of thought create a minefield for students to navigate when isolating the relevant content to leverage in answering a prompt. Less competent students may try to circumvent answering a prompt they are struggling with by providing a list of irrelevant content and fabricating indefensible relationships between them, or simply neglecting to state a relationship at all. In short, the thinking required in performing causation has not happened. See the example provided below:

Too focused on extraneous details: "What was an effect of the Columbian Exchange?"

Student Response: *The Columbian Exchange was when the Old World and the New World started trading after Columbus discovered the Americas with his three ships, the Nina, the Pinta, and the Santa Maria. They traded ideas, diseases like smallpox, crops like tomatoes, and animals like horses. The New World changed a lot because of it.*

Note that in the above example, the student never actually answers the question asked. They haven't listed any specific *effects* of the Exchange. The student simply claims there were effects, which is in essence copying assertions from the prompt. The student has responded by recording extraneous facts about the Exchange itself. Unfortunately, even high achieving students will be encouraged to do this because previous teachers have given them high marks for knowing details about an era, even when they haven't shown complex mastery of the causal relationships of history. Refer back to the section "Teaching the Students" for the example of a good response to this prompt. It is also worth noting that the good response is only one sentence and has fewer recalled facts; but it directly responds to the question asked and so better displays the thinking skill. The solution is to have the student become consciously focused on leveraging the formula to assess what the prompt is specifically asking them to provide and what argument will directly respond to the question asked.

Student Misconception 2: English semantics

The English language can provide confusing syntax for students trying to understand causal relationships. Not only is the "how" completely ignored in working out the language for cause and effect, but often in English, the effect is listed before the cause, creating confusion. Consider the following phrases: "due to", "because" "therefore", and "as a result." These signal words all denote a causal relationship is being shown but force the students to record their thoughts out of chronological order. With both "due to" and "because" each phrase grammatically lists the *effect* before the *cause*, creating a challenge as to where the *how* would fit in the three-part model of causation. While, "therefore" and "as a result" both provide language that allows the cause to initiate the effect, there's no room in even this more straightforward iteration that allows for the author to determine where he might include an explanation of the "how' before or after the other elements. Thus, a focus on teaching the students the formula is imperative to overcome the issues of language mechanics so that they can be flexible in their writing based on a solid understanding of their argument.

To help students overcome this challenge of disordered elements, make them aware that the syntax might be confusing so that they can actively try to decode it. In addition, provide students with opportunities to practice using the formula in different orders. It is helpful to provide students with sentence stems that they can utilize with the formula. For example, an appropriate sentence stem for non-chronological argumentation is: "(effect) because (cause) due to (how)" or "(effect) was a result of (cause) which (how)." A response utilizing scaffolding can be seen in the samples used previously regarding the Columbian Exchange, which has also been provided below:

Student Response: *The dramatic drop in Native American population in the 16th century* (effect) *was a result of the Spaniards unknowingly introducing smallpox to the Americas* (cause) *which killed the Natives in record numbers because they had virtually no immunity to the disease* (how).

For those students who continue to struggle with English syntax and causation, guide them to use language that will construct their response in chronological order following the more basic order of the formula. Encouraging the use of sentence stems such as "(cause) so (how). Therefore (effect)" or "(cause) leading to (how) so then (effect)" helps students organize their thoughts and reduces the use of extraneous details as fillers. Other suggested connecting words could be "resulting in", "creates", "thus", "led to", etc. On the next page is an example of this more simply ordered structure from the Columbian Exchange:

> **Student Response:** *The Spaniards unknowingly introduced smallpox to the Americas* (cause) *leading to the death of the Natives in record numbers because they had virtually no immunity to the disease* (how) *so there was a dramatic drop in Native American population in the 16th century* (effect).

After students are more familiar with the formula for and order of the causation skill, only then should they employ more complex patterns of cause and effect language. Students should focus on the reader easily understanding their writing. They need to let go of "sounding smart" and be confident that the evidence of their thinking in social studies is just as impressive when plainly communicated. It will be helpful to remind students often that complexity comes from the level of their thinking and the quality of their argument, not an impressive vocabulary.

Student Misconception 3: Student ability and confidence

Student prior knowledge is critical to take into consideration in assessing mastery of new content. If students have had minimal opportunities to practice higher order thinking skills, they will struggle more with prompts that require these skills. Teaching thinking is always challenging, but particularly for those students who lacked professional or analytical modeling in their personal lives, they will struggle to learn abstract thinking by themselves. If this is the case, the students must be overtly *taught* these skills, because there is so little prior knowledge to *refine*. Patience and understanding are a necessity as it will take time for such students to develop their abstract thinking.

Particularly with causation, where students have been told that they are doing this skill correctly throughout their academic careers, underachieving and overachieving students will both face confidence issues. When students are advanced, but have rarely been challenged at an appropriate level, they can struggle with the initial skills instruction, believing they are more proficient than they are. In addition, students who have been told for years they are "smart" may have developed a fixed mindset about their abilities, and so will often respond with resistance to constructive feedback regarding abstract thinking and metacognition. To remedy this concern, it is necessary to offer a significant amount of narrative feedback and tutoring, as well as conveying clearly that developing these skills will take time and effort. It is helpful to remind students, "If your brain does not hurt, you are not doing it right." Students need to be reassured that practice is an integral part of the learning process, and early attempts that are not successful are not equivalent to failure. Encouraging students to develop a growth mindset will help develop the grit necessary to accept that they do not have all the answers and that they may need to work harder to gain mastery. Redefine failure for students by replacing it with language more associated with closer and closer approximations of success with each attempt made.

Importance of Causation

For students who have not yet learned how to explain relationships between events, seeing it outlined in a graphic organizer can help them visualize *all* the parts of the argument, and help them remember each of the critical components. It can also help them feel less overwhelmed. It makes students more confident if they have a "game plan" regarding how to answer questions. Particularly for the students who have issues with recall, using a formula will help them brainstorm potential answers to the prompt.

Causation is not only one of the first skills humans experience but is also one of the most significant over the course of a lifetime. As students adjust to college level expectations, some can be paralyzed with insecurity over their professor's feedback on their work. If they understand that there is a causal relationship between improved work and improved grades, they will have more confidence altering their performance on future assignments. Likewise, accurately assessing the process for settling a newborn who is crying by studying strategies that work and their level of effectiveness, this may actually save many marriages. Even in professional life, if the effect one wants to achieve is a promotion, there are certain steps that need to be taken in order to achieve that end result, thus attempts to get a promotion require constant use of causation. Real life applications of the cause and effect formula show the causation skill's significance over a lifetime, making it all the more important that it is practiced for mastery in secondary education.

The impact of using causation and practicing higher order thinking skills can best be seen by using the skill itself, to improve how information will be processed and retained. When teaching causation with procedural components included in lessons (*cause*) which allow for connections to be drawn *from* cause *to* effect, deeper understandings develop (*how*) and thus nuanced information can be retained (*effect*). The reality is, analysis is more complex than traditionally taught, even with something as basic as cause and effect. With the introduction of just one skill, a new paradigm for teaching social studies can revolutionize the classroom experience for both teachers and students.

Social Studies Examples by Subject

<u>World Geography prompt</u>:

"How were the Andes Mountains created?"

Cause	How (→)	Effect
Convergent Plate Boundary	Nazca Plate converges on the South American Plate	Andes Mountains
Student Response: *The Andes Mountains are created by a Convergent Plate Boundary as the Nazca Plate converges on the South American Plate and through subduction, the pressure pushes the crust upwards to create mountains.*		

<u>World History prompt</u>:

"What caused the rise of the National Socialist Party in Germany in the 1930s?"

Cause	How (→)	Effect
Treaty of Versailles	Hyperinflation and resentment toward the Allies and the Nazis offered Nationalism and economic hope	Rise of the National Socialist Party
Student Response: *The Nazi party offered solutions to hyperinflation and the hardships imposed on Germany under the Treaty of Versailles, so Germans felt hope again in overcoming their economic difficulties as well as a new sense of nationalism; thus, the National Socialist party rose to prominence.*		

<u>United States History prompt</u>:

"What caused the American Revolution?"

Cause	How (→)	Effect
Salutary Neglect	Colonies were used to self-government and colonists felt their rights were being taken away and Britain was tyrannical	The American Revolution
Student Response: *The organized resistance against the tyrannical British government in the American Revolution was caused by a history of salutary neglect that allowed the colonies to practice self-governance since their inception, so frustration and resentment arose when the crown reversed the policy and began to impose authority over the colonies.*		

Government prompt:

"Why did the founding fathers create an executive branch in the Constitution?"

Cause	How (→)	Effect
The Articles of Confederation were too weak	Massachusetts struggled to put a stop to Shay's Rebellion because of the lack of a strong central government and executive branch	Executive branch: Article II of the Constitution

Student Response: *The founding fathers created an executive branch in the Constitution in order to address weaknesses inherent in the Articles of Confederation which were highlighted by an inability to respond to early rebellions, such as Shay's Rebellion. This type of upheaval threatened the security of the confederacy resulting in the call for a stronger central government including a stronger executive branch as evidenced by Article II of the Constitution.*

Economics prompt:

"How does an increase in donut supply affect the demand in the marketplace?"

Cause	How (→)	Effect
Supply increases	Price decreases	Quantity demanded increases

Student Response: *When more donut makers enter the marketplace, an increase in the supply of donuts will occur; this lowers the price of all donuts and increases the quantity of donuts demanded.*

Psychology prompt:

"How does positive reinforcement encourage learning?"

Cause	How (→)	Effect
Positive Reinforcement	Provide a positive stimulus as a reward after each preferred behavior.	The person or animal will start to exhibit the preferred behavior more often.

Student Response: *Positive reinforcement helps encourage learning by providing a positive stimulus as a reward after a preferred behavior is exhibited so a person or animal will learn to repeat the preferred behavior more often through continued reinforcement.*

Causation (c/e) Reflection

At this point, take a moment to reflect on the causation skill and practice some metacognition. It is tempting to take revelations from this first skill and dive into the next chapter without allowing for meaningful application and analysis. Remember, it is essential that each skill is practiced in isolation by the instructor and students to internalize it's use before additional skills can be effectively added. Arguably, causation will be the easiest skill to teach and is a great place to start with students before introducing more complex skills. Here are some reflective questions to get started:

1. How has your understanding of causation changed after reading this chapter?

2. What do you think your students' reaction will be to these new revelations about cause and effect?

3. Where do you anticipate your students having the most misunderstandings and what scaffolding will they need when introduced to the skill?

4. What steps do you need to take to increase your confidence in generating and grading causation prompts?

5. How will you implement the causation skill in a lesson in your classroom?

Chapter 5:

Comparison (c/c)

Skill Overview
      Comparison is another building block skill that is critical to the development of historical thinking skills. It is finding the similarities and differences between two topics and drawing a conclusion after critical analysis. A Venn diagram is just the first step of comparison; students must also be able to describe the similarities and differences they see in the table which is higher level abstract thinking. Finally, the students must draw a conclusion that answers a prompt or is an original thought about the comparison made.

How To
      Step 1: Create a comparison table or a Venn diagram
      Step 2: Describe the similarities and differences
      Step 3: Organize into a 1-2 sentence conclusion

Graphic Organizer

Step 1	TOPIC 1	Similarities	TOPIC 2
Step 2	Analysis - Describe Similarities and Differences		
Step 3	Conclusion		

Sentence Stems
TOPIC 1 and TOPIC 2 are similar in who/what/when/where/why/how/etc they ...
      (Can also use SPICE or other descriptors as students advance.)
TOPIC 1 and TOPIC 2 are different in who/what/when/where/why/how/etc they ...
      TOPIC 1 is....
      TOPIC 2 is....
In conclusion...

Example
A sheet cake and cupcakes can both be distributed easily at parties and allow many loved ones to celebrate a major event, yet cupcakes are easier to clean up after since each is wrapped individually, you don't need utensils to serve or eat them, nor plates to distribute them.

Introduction to Comparison

Comparison is another skill that students typically think will be easy for them, but in reality, it requires more abstract thinking than is regularly taught. They take for granted that their thinking process does not need to be articulated in defense of their argument because students traditionally believe they have finished the thinking by making a list of characteristics. Comparison, similarly to causation, has three components; yet it is unlikely students will appreciate the final component because it is not frequently taught intentionally. Comparison is also a skill learned in early childhood, but often only superficially. For example, siblings could learn to compare by debating different breakfast cereals. The children figure out what characteristics they like or don't like about each cereal and then must compare those characteristics in order to argue which is better. Yet, this critical argumentation stage is often halted by the parent, before it is concluded successfully. At least nine research-based studies conducted over the past decade have proven that comparing topics is one of the best ways to learn and encode information (Marzano, 2019a). Therefore, our goal as educators is to capitalize on this inherent benefit.

How the Skill Works

Teaching comparison can be particularly tricky because of the variety of terminology used when asking for the skill such as similarities, differences, compare, and contrast. To simplify, focus on the three distinct steps in the process of performing this historical thinking skill. First, one must compare similarities by identifying and describing repeating characteristics in each topic. Second, one must compare differences, or dissimilarities, by identifying and describing contrasting characteristics in each topic. Finally, one must draw an original conclusion about the extent to which the topics are similar or different. It's this final step that tends to be underrepresented in instruction.

When one compares items, no matter how simple or complex, often the final step in the process where an abstract conclusion is drawn is neglected. Many students are taught early on that the simple act of listing characteristics can stand on its own. Both the listing of characteristics and an analysis of them are necessary to perform comparison. Most often comparison is taught with a simple T-chart model that overlooks similarities, focusing solely on differences, or students are given a Venn diagram or a comparison table and asked to list similarities and differences. In both cases, this step is really only Lower Bloom's activities in that the students are at most simply recalling and understanding information, particularly if they are using reference material because the students only need to identify elements of each topic and no conclusion is explored. For example, say someone needs to compare taking a a taxi or a bus to their destination. On the next page is a comparison chart of considerations.

Taxi	Bus
can drop you off at the door cost dependent on distance traveled just you and the taxi driver	would drop you off two blocks from the door flat rate fee for ride traveling with multiple other passengers
Similarities	
have a professional driver and passengers will need to wait 10 minutes for it to arrive someone else owns the vehicle	

Step one is listing attributes of each topic and often, if assigned in a classroom, students can and will just copy from their class notes to fill out a table such as the one above. In order to perform a complete comparison and help students retain what they've learned by comparing, the students need to draw conclusions about, or *describe* what they have deduced in addition to listing. Identifying characteristics for a chart is simply a requirement to begin comparing, but comparison itself is incomplete without drawing independent conclusions about the features listed by describing the patterns assessed. Thus, the students need to understand that the Venn Diagram is just step one in the analyzing process.

The next step in comparison is to describe the pattern amongst the similarities and differences listed in step one. For example, drawing an acceptable conclusion about similarities would be, "*The taxi and the bus are similar in that they are both modes of public transportation.*" In order to describe a difference, students need to identify specifically what is thematically different between the topics. For example, it was noted that the taxi could drop a passenger at the door of his destination while the bus would drop him off two blocks from his destination. Acceptable answers in this case would be, "*The taxi and the bus are different in where they would drop off the passenger.*" The *thematic* difference is location of the drop off, so that is the conclusion the student would draw. Following the sentence description, the student can then go more in depth about the details of what they are comparing in a recall format.

The third step in comparison is to draw an original conclusion that answers a prompt. When taught, the prompt should be given to the students at the beginning of the activity so that they can focus on the themes of the prompt in their analysis.

Example Prompt: "Is the bus or the taxi the best way to get to the restaurant?"

> **Student Response**: *While both the bus and a taxi would require a ten-minute wait, the taxi is the best way to get to the restaurant because it will drop off the passenger at the door which is more efficient transportation than the bus.*

As with all other skills, once the students see how the formula works with an authentic example, the next step is to apply the skill formula to content.

One of the most beneficial strategies for impressing on the students the importance of practicing metacognition is to remind them that they are doing most of these skills every day, they just are not aware of it. The reason to practice these skills is to make them more aware of what their brain is doing so that they can learn to perform abstract thinking on command. To highlight how familiar students are with the thinking skills in their daily lives, and to draw their attention to the academic implications of this natural life-experience thinking is to hypothesize a real-life choice and use it to perform metacognition.

Consider the following scenario: "Should I take a date to prom or go with friends?" In considering with whom one might want to spend a milestone social event, one might consider a host of different criteria. But the criteria will all center around a comparison, never actually recorded, that ends with a conclusion answering the question they didn't even know they asked themselves: how can I maximize my benefits (in this case enjoyment of the social event)? This is what makes this skill so challenging for students. The final step of comparison is often overlooked because in daily life when this skill is used the final step is rarely recorded. It is instead executed. The decision is made, and an invitation is issued to the appropriate person with whom one wants to attend the Prom. Although they practice comparison and the conclusions drawn from comparing, they are rarely conscious of the final step, so when asked to translate the skill to an academic application, they tend to skip over this final important component. In short, each comparison, no matter how simple or complicated, requires a conclusion to be drawn or the comparison has not effectively been completed.

Teaching the Students

The most critical task of the teacher for comparison is to communicate the importance of completing the final step of drawing a conclusion. Too often teachers end up with a summary of the listed characteristics and then experience frustration as the teacher is left to assume what the student *meant* to say about that comparison given that the student was never overtly trained, nor asked to describe or conclude. As an educator, high expectations regarding critical thinking skills requires clear communication about how to perform abstract thinking. This is one reason to ensure the frequent use of planned scaffolding and anchor charts to communicate consistently, such as the one provided below:

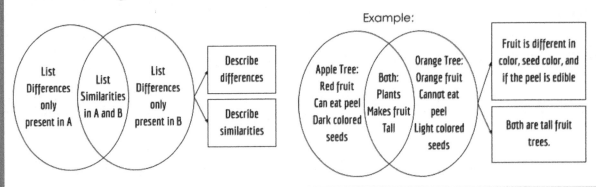

Comparison (c/c)

Student can discern that comparison is being assessed in a prompt and accurately respond by isolating and describing similarities and differences.

When first introducing the comparison skill it is important to clarify that students are prone to overconfidence and will often think they have completed the task of comparing before they draw their conclusions. If the art of thoroughly comparing does not come naturally to students, they will need significant amounts of scaffolding. With less experienced students, start with some very structured sentences until they learn through repetition a format for comparison. Students particularly struggle with identifying the indicator they are contrasting or do not ensure that the contrast is in regards to the same criteria. In this case, the teacher should prompt the students: Are the items being compared different in who they are? What they are doing? When they are? Where they are? Why they are? Or how they are doing something? This gives the students a list of topics to consult in order to find a quality comparison. An effective resource to use for scaffolding is providing sentence stems for students to leverage in early attempts at comparison such as the ones offered below:

TOPIC 1 *and* TOPIC 2 *are* <u>similar</u> *in who/what/when/where/why/how/etc they ...*
TOPIC 1 *and* TOPIC 2 *are* <u>different</u> *in who/what/when/where/why/how/etc they ...*
TOPIC 1 *is....*
TOPIC 2 *is....*
In conclusion...

The next step of complexity would be to offer students comparisons leveraging themes of the social sciences. For example, ask the students if the characteristics are different economically, politically, socially, etc. A common acronym used in social studies classes is SPICE. SPICE stands for society, politics, interactions with the environment, culture, and the economy. Once the student is proficient at utilizing the sentence stems and identifying and describing similarities and differences, they can use this skill to draw a conclusion and eventually apply this skill in thesis writing for essays. For more information on essay argumentation and thesis writing see Chapter 11.

In applying this concept to social sciences content, a ready example can be found in comparisons of the United States, and the United Soviet Socialist Republic during the Cold War era. When introducing content to this skill, remind the students of each step and model the process with this less familiar and less authentic content. The first step for the students is to create a comparison table or a Venn Diagram that includes information that is on the theme of the prompt topic as seen below:

Example Prompt: <u>"Compare the significance of the United States and the Soviet Union regarding their international influence in the Cold War era."</u>

Topic One	Topic Two
Soviet Union • Communist economy • Communist government • Warsaw Pact	**United States** • Capitalist economy • Democratic Republic government • NATO
Similarities	
• Participated in proxy wars • Sought to expand their principle ideologies globally • Used 3rd world countries to increase geopolitical power	

Then the students should practice applying the comparison from the graphic organizer to the prompt with sentence stems. In this case they are focusing on analyzing facts about both countries on the theme of international influence to "describe". As the formulas are learned, students will be able to mentally practice the early steps of comparison and move more fluidly through all three steps of comparison. See the description sentences on the next page that utilize the provided sentence stems:

> **Student Response:** *The Soviet Union and the United States are **similar** in their use of proxy wars to advance their economic and political agendas in third world countries. The Soviet Union and the United States are **different** in their organization of international alliance groups. The Soviet Union created the Warsaw Pact from their satellite countries already under their control. The United States helped found NATO through an alliance with other very powerful and autonomous democracies.*

The third, and most difficult step for students is to formulate a conclusion that responds to the prompt. See an example conclusion in the box below:

> **Student Response:** *Although both the US and the USSR sought to influence third world countries, the Soviet Union used dependent satellite countries already included in their Soviet Republic to create the illusion of a powerful alliance, while the United States created a true alliance of interdependence among independent and sovereign democracies ultimately wielding and leveraging more international influence.*

Troubleshooting

Student Misconception 1: Specificity

The most common issue that students will have with the comparison skill is they will not be specific enough in their answers. This is usually because they do not remember the content or do not understand the question. Perhaps the students are also not familiar with high expectations for intellectual arguments and have previously been allowed to give generalized answers to prompts and still earn high marks for completion. Given the Cold War example, an ineffective response to that prompt might be:

> **Student Response:** *The Soviet Union and the United States are similar in that they are countries. They are different in money.*

This response not only states only the obvious, but also fails to prove mastery of the information or the effective use of the comparison skill. It is important to continuously establish high expectations in writing by modeling specificity as well as sharing and explaining good peer examples for the class. In addition, it is often effective to refine students' academic understanding of the antithesis of specificity, the word "vague". By highlighting what "vague" means, students can learn what needs to be done to fix their work based on narrative feedback. See Chapter 3 for discussion on the importance of narrative feedback. Students need to practice substituting more specific language on command by rewriting their vague work in order to make specificity and nuance in writing a habit.

Student Misconception 2: Describing vs. listing

One of the most difficult tasks in teaching the metacognition of comparison is to ensure the students understand the difference between "describing" and "listing" as academic actions. Students must be able to understand the difference between these two actions so that they can perform each of them as required. For more discussion on task verbs see Chapter 2. Listing is recall and does not show understanding or mastery of content, so it cannot be used in isolation without a clear conclusion. In contrast, describing requires higher level thinking than simple recall as understanding the content is a prerequisite to describing two ideas in one cohesive phrase. Therefore, the students are asked to describe similarities and differences and include the evidence to support that description which inherently has them recalling and leveraging facts. In this way, content is not lost due to a skills based focus, instead it is learned more deeply. Below are two responses from a student, but only one describes.

Evidence of analysis using content
Describing: *The Soviet Union and the United States were different in what type of economy they used. (The student can then use a list of information as evidence to support this claim)*

Evidence of familiarity with content
Listing: *The Soviet Union and the United States were different in that the Soviet Union had a communist economy and the United States was capitalist. (This claim will be more difficult to elaborate on without repetition and redundancy)*

When first looking at these two example responses, it is all too easy to assess that the second answer is the stronger answer because of the number of facts included. However, analysis requires not just a listing of characteristics, but a conclusion to be drawn in a description as well. An educator focused on critical thinking will find that the response that provides more evidence of analysis is the first response. In the comparison skill, describing is an original idea from the student that exhibits an understanding by highlighting a relevant characteristic from both topics as one cohesive phrase. In the first example, the description was "the type of economy they used." Listing, on the other hand, is a collection of information that hasn't been processed using the student's thinking skills.

The second example is therefore, while specific, a simple regurgitated list of previously established facts that the Soviet Union was communist and the United States was capitalist. The student properly comparing would use this information to support their description, not rely on it to solely be the answer recorded as was seen in the second example. The sentence stems presented in the "Teaching the Students" section of this chapter force students to metacognitively do two separate actions, describing first *and then* listing, with the same information leveraged as evidence. If students struggle with the sentence stems they are struggling with their abstract thinking. Sentence stems provide mental boundaries, like training wheels, for ensuring the skill and specific verb task is being performed thoroughly and accurately, until the thinking skills become habits of mind.

Student Misconception 3: Contrasting without a strategy

Planning an argument, as most teachers can attest, is one of the most overlooked steps by students in critical thinking, especially those students who are overconfident, often convinced they have already mastered skills with which they still need much practice to perform competently. Lack of planning skills is most evident when a student attempts to describe differences and instead lists disconnected ideas, as seen below:

Student Responses:

Example 1: The Soviet Union is communist and the United States was in NATO.

Example 2: The Soviet Union is communist and the US is not.

Identifying a similarity inherently forces students to identify a pattern in the characteristics of the topics, but the differences are often much trickier. Students often assume differences don't need to be aligned, due to the very nature of the characteristics being different. What students end up submitting is a list of random differences or disconnected topics, as seen in Example 1. They do not take into account any particular theme paralleled with the characteristics being compared for their differences, a step necessary to create a description. Instead of picking the theme of government for a description, the student provides one fact about government and one about alliances, which are not parallel - a necessity in contrasting.

Thematic considerations can be of help to the student in finding parallelism, as seen in the provided sentence stems in "Teaching the Students" section. Early scaffolding for describing tasks forces the students to pick a theme to compare using who, what, when, where, or why two topics are different. Themes of social studies can also be used to leverage categories of characteristics, such as social, cultural, political, or economic, to help students find parallelism.

Another mistake students often make, as shown in Example 2, is to contrast two topics by declaring that the absence of a characteristic is a difference. The negation of a characteristic is not applicable as valid evidence in argumentation. Students must ensure that parallelism is employed, which requires contrasting characteristics.

Student Misconception 4: Blindness to subtlety

The students struggle to do both tasks of comparing similarities and contrasting differences most when the topics to analyze are remarkably similar or very different. If the topics are exceedingly similar or are drastically different, the students become so focused on what they find to be the most obvious characteristics, that they struggle with further analysis. In short, the students may struggle to find subtle differences or be blinded to similarities once they develop tunnel vision for the characteristics they see most readily. Repetition of the expectation to compare both similarities and differences with every topic will encourage students to keep an open mind when analyzing for comparisons. In addition, encourage students by providing positive feedback even for small steps toward success to build confidence in their arguments and responses, no matter how subtle or different from their peers. Mistakes in thinking cost little as repeated attempts can be employed to further advance students toward mastery.

Importance of Comparison

Comparison is one of the best tools for historians to use, particularly in the classroom, since it operates as a lab with dead people as the tools. In addition, mastery of comparison is a necessary step in more complex analysis which will be discussed in later chapters. Without mastery of these early foundational analytical skills, more abstract analysis will seem insurmountable.

History lends itself to comparison so readily it is almost impossible to avoid. Consider something as complex as Harry S. Truman's decision to employ the atomic bomb in World War II. As contemporary students grapple with the consequences of his choice, it is worthwhile to analyze how Truman made the choice through comparison. Truman had to compare the potential of the atomic bomb to more traditional war making, such as planning a land invasion of Japan, in order to execute a decision. A list of concerns Truman had to weigh might include such characteristics of war as costs, both in financial terms, and in terms of human life, risk factors and uncertainty levels. In order to make such an important decision, Truman had to be proficient at comparison by contrasting the relative costs of different strategies to effectively end the war in the Pacific. Comparison must be employed in order to learn from the past. Indeed, comparison is the crystal ball of history.

Human beings are profit maximizers. People make decisions in their own best interest. But each decision made inherently requires comparison. Knowing this, the comparison skill can be used to teach students about decision making processes using much safer content than when they will be using this skill to determine whether or not to commit to a 30-year mortgage. By teaching comparison well, students will make better decisions about which college to attend, how much debt they are willing to accrue to go to college, or what alternative career avenue they may pursue. Comparing effectively will offer students, parents, teachers, and truly society at large, better peace of mind and confidence about the future. Using comparison, students can investigate the thought process of some of the most historically significant leaders, actions, and events, for good or for ill, and allow them to practice a critical skill that transcends not only the discipline of history, but the classroom itself, providing valuable support well into their adult lives.

Social Studies Examples by Subject

<u>World Geography prompt</u>:

"Compare the Andes Mountains and the Rocky Mountains as physical barriers."

Step 1	**Andes** • South America • Terrace farming • 45 million years old	**Similarities** • Created by converging plate boundaries with subduction	**Rockies** • North America • Mining • 80-55 million years old
Step 2	**Analysis:** The Andes and Rocky Mountains are different in how old they are. The Andes Mountains are 45 million years old and very tall and steep. The Rocky Mountains are 55-80 million years old and much more eroded and wider. These mountain ranges are similar in that they were both created by a convergent subduction plate boundary.		
Step 3	**Student Response:** *While both ranges were created with a convergent subduction boundary, the Andes Mountains are more of a physical barrier to humans than the Rocky Mountains because they are much steeper and younger, therefore more difficult to cross.*		

<u>World History prompt</u>:

"Compare the European Theatre and the Pacific Theatre of action in WWII regarding their complexity of execution."

Step 1	**European Theatre** • First point of allied invasion • Multiple foes • Close borders	**Similarities** • Use of airplanes • Fought by the United States • Nationalism	**Pacific Theatre** • Island hopping • Japanese determination • Atomic bomb used
Step 2	**Analysis:** The European and Pacific Theatres were different in how many countries were involved in the fighting. In the Pacific Theatre, most of the fighting was between two countries, the United States and Japan. In the European Theatre, the Allied and Axis alliances saw coordination between multiple friends against multiple foes. These theatres were similar in that the United States fought in both.		
Step 3	**Student Response:** *The fighting in Europe required more cohesive Allied efforts and cooperation than was seen in the Pacific Theatre, which was predominantly characterized by US actions, therefore the European Theatre of war was more complex.*		

United States History prompt:

"Compare the perspectives of the Loyalists and Patriots during the American Revolution."

Step 1	Loyalists	Similarities	Patriots
	• Wanted British citizenship benefits • Anglican • Influenced by monarchical ideals	• Wanted their businesses to thrive • Wanted to minimize loss of life	• Wanted self-governance • Deists • Influenced by Enlightenment ideals
Step 2	**Analysis:** The Loyalists and Patriots were different in which movements influenced their political ideology. The Loyalists were much more conservative and relied strongly on British monarchical ideas. The Patriots were more progressive and were influenced by new Enlightenment ideals about representation and human rights. The Patriots and the Loyalists were similar in that they both felt like they were fighting to ensure their businesses stayed profitable. The Loyalists wanted to continue capitalizing on relationships with Parliament to make money and the Patriots wanted more autonomy in business choices.		
Step 3	**Student Response:** *Although both the Patriots and the Loyalists actively sought to ensure profitability for their businesses, the disagreement over preferred systems of government rule was the primary dividing force in society during the American Revolution.*		

Government prompt:

"Compare the prestige associated with being a Congressmen in the House of Representatives to that of being a Senator."

Step 1	House	Similarities	Senate
	• 435 members • Represent districts • Elected every 2 years	• Both representative of select constituency and dependent on re-election	• 100 members • Represent states • Elected every 6 years
Step 2	**Analysis:** The House of Representatives and the Senate are different in who they represent. The House of Representatives represents districts based on population within states, so that the number of representatives per state is proportional to population. The Senate represents the states as a whole through equal representation. These congresses are similar in that all representatives are dependent on re-election.		
Step 3	**Student Response:** *While all Congressmen represent their constituents, the Senate is more prestigious than the House due to the terms of their elections and the limited seats available.*		

Economics prompt:

"Does supply or demand have a bigger impact in the marketplace?"

Step 1	Supply	Similarities	Demand
	• Taxes • Technology • Resource costs	Influenced by • Expectation • number of other players in market • prices of other goods	• Tastes • Preferences • Income
Step 2	**Analysis:** Supply and demand are different in their role in the product market. Supply is associated with the making of products. Demand is associated with the purchasing of products. They are similar in that their actions in the marketplace are influenced by expectation, number of other players in the market, and prices of other goods.		
Step 3	**Student Response:** *While there are significant overlaps in determinants of players in the marketplace, according to Classical economists, supply's dependency on resource costs in order to produce goods to meet the consumer's demand typically has a greater impact on the marketplace than demand itself.*		

Psychology prompt:

"To what extent are the processes of classical and operant conditioning similar?"

Step 1	Classical	Similarities	Operant
	• Involves reflexes and respondent behavior • Reactions to unconditioned stimuli are associated which trigger behavior	• Associative learning that controls human behavior • Requires repetition • Behaviorism	• Involves chosen behaviors • Behaviors associated with consequences that will increase or decrease behavior
Step 2	**Analysis:** Classical and operant conditioning are different in what type of behaviors are being affected. Classical conditioning involves reflexive and respondent behaviors. Operant conditioning involves chosen behaviors. These conditioning systems are similar in that they both require repetition to acquire association.		
Step 3	**Student Response:** *Although operant and classical conditioning address different types of behaviors, they are similar in process to a large extent because of the repetition of associations to modify behavior.*		

Comparison (c/c) Reflection

At this point, take a moment to reflect on the comparison skill and practice some metacognition. Remember, it is essential that each skill is practiced in isolation by the instructor and students to internalize it's use before additional skills can be effectively added. Here are some reflective questions to get started:

1. How has your understanding of comparison changed after reading this chapter?

2. What do you think your students' reaction will be to these new revelations about similarities and differences?

3. What do you predict will be most common misconception about comparison in your classroom? What troubleshooting technique will address it best?

4. What steps do you need to take to increase your confidence in generating and grading causation prompts?

5. How will you implement the comparison skill in a lesson in your classroom?

Chapter 6:

Contextualization (c/x)

Skill Overview

Contextualization is arguably one of the most fundamental historical thinking skills. When studying history, contextualization is constantly performed informally as one generates background information to mentally situate the topic being analyzed so that the resulting analysis is informed regarding place and time of occurrence. Contextualization can also be written more formally to set the stage, or provide background, for written analysis. In both cases, contextualization is generating topically and thematically relevant information, including big themes and relevant details, to a subject and then connecting the information through the highlighting of its significance.

How To

> Type 1: Informing Analysis - used constantly (informal)
>> Step 1: generate lots of information regarding a topic
>> Step 2: connect most relevant information in terms of theme and scope
> Type 2: Setting the stage - used to introduce an essay (formal)
>> Step 3: Explain relevant big themes and details
>> Step 4: Explain connection to prompt

Graphic Organizer

Big Themes (Thematic Organization)	Specific Details	Significance to Topic (Scope of Topic)
Conclusion		

Sentence Stems

For setting the stage:

1st sentence: Before the (topic) (big theme in history) was happening during (era or time period).
2nd sentence: This is seen in (specific evidence examples).
3rd sentence: (Big theme) led to (topic) because...

Example

While most cakes tend to celebrate major life events, birthday cakes tend to be more understated than wedding cakes due to the importance of the event, the fact that a wedding often happens only one time as opposed to every year, and the number of people to be served from it is decidedly greater.

Introduction to Contextualization

Once learned, contextualization can feel like a natural skill for adults, so some teachers assume it should be easily learned and executed by students. However, because contextualization is often learned unconsciously from both modeling and trial and error, many adults do not recognize when they are doing the skill or the metacognition that occurred to enable it to be seamlessly provided. Trouble arises when there is a student who is not able to make the unconscious leap to understanding the role of context and its application independently, because adults are often not able to explain how to do it. Even when students do become familiar with context's characteristics as a skill, there are still significant opportunities for missteps in execution when they struggle to make or capture abstract leaps in ideas. Like all skills previously discussed, context is also deceptive as it has two distinct roles that are often underutilized by students and are much more purposeful than is commonly believed.

How the Skill Works

The reality is contextualization is constantly utilized when practicing the social studies discipline. In short, it is situating topics within a broader relevant framework to provide significance in analysis. This invaluable skill is used unconsciously every day, and when done inaccurately or when missing, it is obvious an error has been made. Thus, the students must learn to consciously and purposefully provide context. For example, if a student asks, "Was the due date Thursday or Friday?" the teacher should recognize right away that they are not able to answer the question because the student did not provide any framework, or context, for their question. In this case, the context could be about a daily assignment given in class that day, a longer-term project students have been working on for several weeks, or about an extra-curricular responsibility for which the instructor is a club sponsor. If the teacher attempts to answer the question as is, there is a strong likelihood that their response will not be a relevant one or address the question the student *meant* to ask. In other words, no significance was provided so the teacher cannot analyze the question to answer it. To become more proficient, students first need to understand the varied uses of this skill including its informal function of *informing analysis* and its formal manifestation in *setting the stage* for analysis. These two uses for context should be dealt with separately so as to distinguish the varied uses for this skill.

Context must be kept in mind when studying any subject so that it can inform analysis. In fact, this skill is so embedded in the discipline that it is impossible to think historically and not be contextualizing; however, it is possible to contextualize wrong. Every person, place, issue, and event that is to be discussed can be understood only through the context of the circumstances surrounding the discussion of each topic. When a topic is embedded successfully in context, deeper understandings of the historical circumstance can come to light and analysis is strengthened. In this way, using the context skill to inform analysis is an informal function as it is inherently a part of historical discussions and embedded in the discourse associated with any series of events or topics allowing for significance to emerge when employed successfully.

For example, in just one average day in the history classroom, context informed analysis occurs constantly. In class, students must remember what was learned the previous day as context for the current lesson, then the students need to remember what has already been taught in the lecture as context for the other information provided, and any formative or summative assessment given would require the students to contextualize each question in the framework of what has been taught. Political cartoons can also prove difficult to analyze without first contextualizing the events and references occurring in the picture and text. In practice, students are expected to include context on any topic at any time through both broad thematic analysis as well as providing depth of significance.

Contextualization formally manifests when it is used to set the stage for a long essay or document based question. The expectation is that in two to three sentences, students will provide background information on the

> **Logistics of Skill Implementation with Multiple Choice**
>
> "In the College Board Advanced Placement system most of the multiple choice questions are stimulus based, and thus work easily with a skills system. In essence, a source excerpt is used as a reference for three to four questions. Those multiple choice questions ask the students to perform a skill by processing the stimulus through a specific skill to answer the questions. A true skills based classroom should follow this model for multiple choice. At the very least the multiple choice questions should require the students to perform a skill, even if there is not a stimulus attached. However, there are oftentimes scaffolded multiple choice questions that ask the students to perform only Lower Bloom's where they are simply required to regurgitate information to answer the question. Because Lower Bloom's questions ask for some considerably basic application of historical context as students decode and recall only relevant facts, we can consider those questions, even superficially, contextualization for recording purposes. Yet, this "catch all" should be used sparingly. If you find yourself grading contextualization too much, change the nature of the assignments or questions to other skills."
>
> – Toms

topic about which they will write the essay. In those three sentences they need to do two purposeful actions: describe relevant information about the topic at hand and explain *how* the information they provided is relevant to the topic. When students describe relevant information they should provide both *big themes* that are occurring as well as *specific details*. If a student was providing context to the American Civil War, they could provide "sectionalism" and "slavery" as big themes, and "Missouri Compromise of 1820" and "John Brown's Raid on Harper's Ferry" as specific details. The most crucial step in setting the stage, which is often overlooked because it is a part of argumentation and sometimes more difficult, is to explain to the reader how the details provided help build a greater understanding of the historical situation regarding the topic being explored. See the example below, given an essay topic about the American Civil War:

> **Student Response:** *In the 19th century America was experiencing a period of sectionalism, wherein each area of the country was putting their own needs above that of the country as a whole, causing significant tension. One of the things the Northern and Southern sections argued over was the issue of slavery, which manifested in the Compromise of 1820 and John Brown's Raid on Harper's Ferry, both of which can be considered contributing factors to the Civil War. As the Civil War got underway, these sections had long been arguing in congress and violently in the streets before the war had even begun.*

In this example, the first two sentences are focused on providing the big themes and details and the third sentence focuses specifically on connecting the information provided to the topic of the essay. While context is constantly utilized as an informal function to inform analysis throughout the essay writing process, the skill of using context to set the stage for an essay is a formal manifestation that is oftentimes graded and can be more easily taught with more obvious scaffolding.

The skill of contextualization requires students to consider a variety of background knowledge and then to decide which information is the most relevant to providing significance. Regardless of whether the student is informing analysis or setting the stage, contextualization needs to be considered in terms of the general thematic organization as well as the more specific scope of a topic. See the table below:

Context Considerations		Examples
Thematic organization (breadth)	Social, political, intellectual, interactions with the environment, cultural, economic, geographic, etc.	Demographic characteristics of Progressives; socio-economic class structure of Revolutionists
Scope of topic (depth)	Time and place parameters of topic	Foreign v domestic issues; Antebellum era

These are not subdivisions of contextualization, but instead this is a system to refine the conversation about organizing possible background information. This tool is an excellent springboard to support students as they learn about the underappreciated complexity of using context intentionally.

Teaching the Students

When introducing the concept of context to students, they will often grasp the early definitional quality of the skill, without appreciating its complexities. Examples of "real life" contextualization significantly help students understand what good examples of context look like so they are more apt to recognize when they have or have not conducted the skill effectively.

One relevant example for students to see context in action is in regard to television shows. If someone has waited for a new season to be released, they likely need to refresh their memory regarding the plot and characters. In other words, they need to refresh their context to understand the new season. In fact, the show will likely start the new season with a recap for this very reason: the viewers need a *formal* manifestation of context. However, if a viewer has been binge watching a full season of a show, they will not need to watch a recap as the context is so recently established throughout the season. This also provides an example of the *informal*, but inherent nature of context as a constant practice required from students. When it is done well and consistently, contextualization makes the student's analysis more effective as well as efficient. Once this example is established for students, a teacher can prompt them to provide background information or context, by asking them to finish the phrase: "Previously on…".

As another relevant example when first introducing the *formal* manifestation of context in essay writing, or how to set the stage, is the scrolling text that precedes every Star Wars film. It shows students the effectiveness of providing context as George Lucas primes the audience for the storyline about to play out by recapping what had already transpired in the previous episode in order to establish within what context, or framework, upcoming events will occur. This recap was particularly necessary as the fourth installment of the series was published first, so the audience had no context for the events of the 1977 movie without the three sentences of scrolling text. This concrete example acts as a relevant model to assist students in understanding the importance of setting the stage.

When requiring the "setting the stage" formal manifestation of context in writing exercises, particularly with long essays and document based questions, sentence stems can be provided to lower secondary grade levels or low performers in upper grades. However, sentence stems, like the ones that follow, should only be used in differentiation, as context is best done when it is flexible and focused mostly on providing the thematic framing, specific details, and connections to and within the topic, regardless of the way it is presented.

Context (3 sentences)
- **1st sentence:** Before the (topic) (big theme in history) was happening during (era or time period).
- **2nd sentence:** This is seen in (specific evidence examples).
- **3rd sentence:** (Big theme) led to (topic) because…

See how the sentence stems could be used to build formal context for an introduction paragraph in the example below used with 9th grade World Geography:

Topic	Big Theme	Era or Time Period	Evidence/Details
Gold Rush in California	Industrialization in the Northeast	1800s in America	Overcrowding and poverty in the Northeast

Student Response: *Before the Gold Rush in California, Industrialization was happening during the 1800s in America. This is seen in the urbanization of cities in the Northeast which led to overcrowding and poverty. Industrialization led to the Gold Rush to California because lots of poor people were desperate to make their fortune and start a new life.*

Another technique that is useful for students to continue to keep context awareness and use as a priority is a graphic organizer as an anchor chart in the classroom, as seen below:

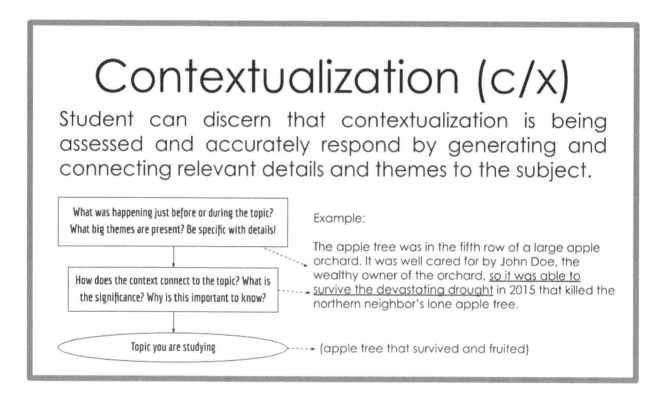

Troubleshooting

Student Misconception 1: Students don't know information

If a student is struggling with context there is a very good chance that their main problem is that they do not know the information about the topic, so they are not able to generate relevant information to frame their response. Usually in this case the student will decide that the skill is too hard and will avoid completing the task. The reality is that the student did not complete the necessary thinking in Lower Bloom's, so they do not understand the information enough to analyze it at a higher level. The student either did not learn the facts so they cannot recall it or did not strive to understand the facts that were presented to them. If that is the case, then the student will be unable to apply the information and will certainly not be able to analyze the topic. The recommendation for students struggling with these lower levels is to provide study skill exposure so they can spend their own time on Lower Bloom's more effectively. Exposure to time management techniques to fit in more studying, refreshers on mnemonic devices, and other study skills will help students overcome their difficulties with knowledge and understanding so they are ready and able to analyze abstractly.

In addition, students will often omit critical context which may limit their overall effectiveness in communicating their ideas. Students tend to believe their audience is already immersed in their subject because *they are* in order to answer the prompt. This makes them believe their audience has made the same assumptions they have before the analysis is offered; so omitting context occurs. By pointing out when students provide context in their everyday lives, teachers can make the need to contextualize more relevant to students. One example is highlighting the fact that when telling a story to friends, students often unconsciously set the stage by explaining where and when an event took place as well as who was in attendance, before launching into an entertaining anecdote. This kind of support and explanation enhances the opportunities for context to be provided in academic work and reduces how often it is overlooked.

Student Misconception 2: Irrelevance of evidence

Occasionally there are students who do not understand that simply because chronologically something happened before the events that need to be discussed and analyzed, does not mean those events are appropriate for providing context. Contextualization has to be specific to the circumstances being analyzed and must inform the audience of the "stage" or background upon which events will play out in the ensuing analysis.

The first common mistake is when students provide information that is too far back in time to provide meaningful significance. If a question requires an analysis of military endeavors during Manifest Destiny in the late 19th century, appropriate context might be the War of 1812 for understanding some of the steps taken in the Mexican American War yet one would not use the French and Indian War to set the stage for the Mexican American War as there is simply no relevance. One recommendation is to remind a student that they keep evidence to a specific time constraint, such as 20 years, or a generation.

The other common mistake students make is that they provide information on a different theme than the topic of the prompt. For example, students will relate international affairs as the context for a domestic issue analysis, or they will submit economic circumstances to a social factors' discussion. To resolve this concern, one technique is to highlight the appropriateness of context to the prompt. When the prompt's themes and scope are considered carefully, the relevance of the context can be more accurate. To ensure accuracy of context, limiting the response to a specific time period and breaking down a prompt are both critical to the success of the context provided in setting the stage and informing analysis.

Student Misconception 3: Difficulty intuiting relevance due to overstimulation

Once students understand the nature of both informal context informing analysis and formal context which sets the stage, scaffolding can be provided to help students who have difficulty making the intuitive leaps required to do context. The two intuitive leaps in abstract thinking that must occur when contextualizing are first *generating* relevant information and then *connecting* information to a topic by providing significance. Both actions will likely need to be scaffolded for the underperforming student.

When students are asked for context on a topic, it can be quite arduous for a student to consider every fact they have learned about a subject and decide what is relevant enough to use. When a prompt overstimulates a student, the amount of relevant information they must recall can be so numerous that it actually becomes more difficult to build an argument. Teaching students to consider the theme and scope of a prompt when they attempt to generate information will help them to isolate and organize the most relevant facts. Students can then analyze all the content for a topic they know and choose the relevant information that is associated with appropriate theme and scope.

One technique for modeling how to effectively connect information to a topic assigned is to ensure contextualization is highlighted during instruction. Teachers need to focus on pointing out the *significance* of context clues to allow students to become astute observers of even the informal role context plays. If context provides significance for connecting information, then this needs to be a purposeful part of instruction requiring connections to be made by the instructor during lessons. There are opportunities to purposefully practice the highlighting of significance in daily warmups, the lesson itself, as well as formative assessments.

Student Misconception 4: Confusion with causation

In previously discussed skills, there are implied expectations within a main skill. In the case of contextualization, oftentimes causation is the best skill to utilize in creating significant connections between the generated themes and facts and the topic at hand. When students realize this connection, they begin to either second guess whether they are doing context correctly or they start writing too much context by focusing on the causation skill inherent in context too thoroughly. The best course of action is to discuss with the students that they may need to consider some causation in order to fully provide contextualization, so that they can thoughtfully implement the skill. One strategy to help students become more comfortable with contextualization is to do student-led mini lessons that purposefully integrate opportunities for instruction on the skill specifically. This provides moments for students to practice setting the stage in classroom activities which can resolve many of the issues discussed in this section.

Another strategy for implementing an effective

Leveraging Unsuccessful Examples

"I find that students can sometimes struggle to see how a particular skill is being performed inaccurately. If all the examples I use in instruction continue to be generated by me and thus exhibit only replicas of how the skill is performed, my students may not be able to effectively see where they made an error except through one-on-one tutoring. What I have done in the past is to take student samples of skills performed poorly on a current assignment and convert them into generic typed examples. That way student anonymity can be maintained, yet actual student samples of errors can be used to highlight common challenges faced by many of my students through whole class instruction. To most effectively leverage the examples, I ask the students to determine what the errors are and how to fix them. In debriefing errors together, my students see challenges faced not only by themselves but also by peers, which normalizes the experience of growing slowly over time. This activity can also highlight specific issues that multiple students have exhibited along with the appropriate corrections in a very relevant and recent context. I find this technique allows my instruction to be refined from year to year as I troubleshoot changes in how I present the skills each year and helps fine tune students' skill understanding."

– Tillotson

differentiation between causation and contextualization is to ensure a limit to the focus on causal factors when providing context. Students need to be informed that they need not provide the dozen or so steps that led to the events being discussed, but offering one or two causal factors reminding students to use the three sentence model for context will help alleviate this issue.

Student Misconception 5: Students answer the prompt in the context

When students are asked to set the stage for an essay, sometimes they will have trouble separating the background of the prompt from the answer to the prompt. If the prompt is asking about causes of World War I, their "setting the stage" sentences should *not* include causes of the war. Instead, the students should focus on previous events such as the Spanish-American War, the Scramble for Africa, or impacts of Industrialization as appropriate. Remind the students that setting the stage is background information to inform the analysis of the essay, it should not answer the essay prompt. If utilizing the television episode recap example previously illustrated, remind students that the topic of the essay is the episode they are about to watch, but the context is limited to only the recap of what happened in previous episodes. Another tactic to help students is to tell them to "brain dump" all of the information they know about the era of the topic before they actually begin answering a prompt. The student can then sift through that information to sort context from evidence to support their analysis and not become so focused on the answer that they lose sight of the framework of the topic.

Importance of Contextualization

Contextualization is a critical component of any communication and there are many subtle places where it is already being practiced that can allow for growth in the intentional use of the skill. However, it can be challenging to do actively and on command, particularly if someone is unfamiliar with the steps required to fully leverage relevant information to inform analysis. When metacognition about contextualization is employed, students can get better at practicing contextualization deliberately. Teachers need to consider first where they are already providing context for students and make it part of the daily discussions in class actively. It will help to be obvious about calling attention to the use of context. In this way teachers can employ the academic language introduced here and make it part of everyday discussion. To do this, implement questions such as: "Can you provide me more context for your question?", "What is the context of the topic we are talking about?", or "How does the context of this topic help us understand what is happening?". Teaching context intentionally will allow both the formal function of contextualization in introductory paragraphs as well as the less obvious, embedded, informal manifestation of contextualization to emerge. If context is taught effectively and practiced thoughtfully in academic settings this skill can then transfer to adult life by minimizing miscommunication, creating clearer and purpose driven discussions, and enhancing effective communication to navigate the many challenges faced in adulthood.

Social Studies Examples by Subject

Based on the nature of the elements of Contextualization, the examples provided below will focus on the formal manifestation of context by setting the stage for each topic.

World Geography topic: Plate Boundaries

Big Themes (Thematic Organization)	Specific Details	Significance to Topic (Scope of Topic)
Plate Tectonics	Pangea Fossil evidence	Creates types of plate boundaries
Student Response: *In Earth's early days all the continents were placed together on a giant continent called Pangea, which we know because of how similar plants and animals are around the world through fossil evidence. Over time the plates under Pangea moved away from each other through a process called Plate Tectonics to create the modern seven continents. Today, various types of plate boundaries continuously move violently throughout the Earth.*		

World History topic: World War II

Big Themes (Thematic Organization)	Specific Details	Significance to Topic (Scope of Topic)
Economic struggles Political Resentments	Treaty of Versailles Great Depression	Economic and political tensions Interwar years
Student Response: *Before the outbreak of WWII, political tension and economic collapse were already creating the circumstances for another great war due to resentments from Germany over the Treaty of Versailles as well as lingering resentment against Germany from the allies of WWI. In addition, a global economic collapse of the worldwide economy from the Great Depression led to hyperinflation in Germany which increased tension that was already mounting between European countries. These factors created significant economic and political tension in Europe during the Interwar years prior to the outbreak of WWII.*		

United States History topic: The American Revolution

Big Themes (Thematic Organization)	Specific Details	Significance to Topic (Scope of Topic)
Salutary neglect Enlightenment	French and Indian War John Locke	Regulation of colonies Self-government

Student Response: *Prior to the American Revolution, the colonies were in a state of salutary neglect but fairly loyal to Parliament. However, both the disregard from Britain and the respect to Britain ended with the French and Indian War. While England was not regulating the colonies during the early colonial years, Enlightenment thinking spread around the colonies, particularly the theories of John Locke, and infused itself in self-government. The era of Revolution began as Britain started regulating its colonies in the aftermath of the French and Indian War after they had grown used to regulating themselves.*

Government topic: Constitutional Federalism

Big Themes (Thematic Organization)	Specific Details	Significance to Topic (Scope of Topic)
Expansion of Federalism Interventionism	13th, 14th, 15th Amendments Civil Rights Act of 1964 Voting Rights Act of 1965	Dual Federalism Creative Federalism Devolution

Student Response: *Before the high point of Federal intervention during LBJ's Great Society, the government had already seen a significant expansion of its powers with Amendments enacted by the Federal Government over states' powers after the Civil War. But as states continued to struggle with equality of implementation regarding the 13th, 14th and 15th Amendments due to Jim Crow laws, the Federal government grew in its interventionist role by enacting such legislation as the Civil Rights Act of 1964 and the Voting Rights Act of 1965. These acts then opened the door to even further expansion of Federalism, only to see devolution of Federalism in successive administrations.*

Economics topic: Keynesian Economic Theory

Big Themes (Thematic Organization)	Specific Details	Significance to Topic (Scope of Topic)
Economic Failure Classical theory	Great Depression Federal Deficit spending Increase in National Debt	Demand stimulation
Student Response: *Before the Great Depression, the US economy had already experienced several versions of market failure in terms of multiple panics through boom-and-bust cycles of business that swept the nation due to what Classical Economists assumed was a natural state of affairs for a capitalist economy. However, with the Great Depression, the US government had to find a way to correct for a global economic panic as a result of supply and demand issues and international exchange consequences. John Maynard Keynes provided a solution through his support of increasing deficit spending and adding to the national debt in peace time at an unprecedented level through Roosevelt's New Deal to stimulate demand and ensure supply would eventually rise due to government spending which gave birth to Keynesian economic theory.*		

Psychology topic: Learned Behaviors

Big Themes (Thematic Organization)	Specific Details	Significance to Topic (Scope of Topic)
Behaviorism	Associative Learning Cognitive Learning	Best frameworks
Student Response: *Learning oftentimes falls under the type of psychology called Behaviorism, or the scientific study of observable behavior as well as the Cognitive perspective, the study of how people acquire, store, and process information. There are two types of learning: associative learning based on responses to a stimulus and cognitive learning through observation rather than experience with a stimulus. While human behavior can be explained through other perspectives, the study of learned behaviors is best understood within these frameworks of theory.*		

Contextualization (c/x) Reflection

At this point, take a moment to reflect on the contextualization skill and practice some metacognition. The next skill is much more complex and requires a proficient understanding of causation, comparison, and contextualization to implement. Remember, it is essential that each skill is practiced in isolation by the instructor and students to internalize it's use before additional skills can be effectively added. Here are some reflective questions to get started:

1. How has your understanding of contextualization changed after reading this chapter?

2. What troubleshooting solutions will be easiest and most effective for your students to implement in peer review and personal revisions?

3. What everyday examples can you use to introduce formal and informal context to your students?

4. What steps do you need to take to increase your confidence in assessing and grading student use of context?

> At this point we strongly encourage readers to pause and practice the skills introduced thus far. The rest of the skills are much more complex and will actively incorporate causation, comparison, and contextualization. Keep in mind that teaching a few skills well is better than teaching all of them poorly.
>
> - Toms and Tillotson

Chapter 7:
Change and Continuity over Time (CCOT)

Skill Overview

Although commonly used in the social sciences, change and continuity over time (CCOT) is much more complex than many believe as it utilizes building block skills for deeper analysis. It not only utilizes *contextualization* for building the "before" and "after", but *causation* in explaining the precipitating factors that led to a development which then creates a change over time. In some ways, CCOT asks to *compare* over time. Similarities over time are continuities. Differences in the "before" and "after" are termed changes. In the end, CCOT asks students to complete complex analysis in their conclusion as they describe the processes in human history that stay the same and those that change.

How To

Step 1: Identify whether it was long term factors or a turning point factor that created a development

Step 2: Identify the "before", the "after", how the factor(s) caused a development, and continuities

Step 3: Organize into a conclusion

Graphic Organizer

Before	Factor(s) and Development *Make sure to include a verb that indicates causation*	After
Continuity		

Sentence Stems

Step 2 Stems:
Before (development), ...
(precipitating factors leading to development), ...
After (development), ...
Yet (continuity), ...

Step 3 Stems:
Due to (development), (topic) (verb) in (process).
Despite (development), (process) remained the same because (continuity).

Example

In childhood, birthday cakes tend to be fanciful and center around a favorite character or theme that is often fleeting; however, over time, birthday cakes, while continuing to be used to celebrate one's birthday, becomes understated, and typically center more around the flavor and number of people to be served.

Introduction to Change and Continuity over Time

When discussing changes in a historical context, educators highlight alterations in patterns of history over time. In fact, the traditional study of history is quite *literally* the study of changes and continuities over time in regard to any one subject. For this reason, this skill is perhaps the most commonly used historical skill in classrooms. However, its nuances are only revealed when employing a metacognitive approach to teaching. If considered at all, continuities over time are descriptions of patterns that remain even after changes are considered. Continuities are critical to the study of history because they offer contradiction and reveal opposing patterns to the changes observed, reflecting the state of humanity. In some ways, continuities tell the story of history in a more revealing way than changes because they highlight the habits of humanity, not the exceptions. Despite continuities' significance, oftentimes changes over time are the primary focus of analysis in the classroom because they are easier for students to isolate independently. However, changes should be utilized as a compliment, not a substitution for continuities. Just as significantly, changes over time reveal man's progression through historical developments. Changes typically mark the cornerstones of historical eras, reveal evolutions in ideas and behaviors, and record technological advancements. Indeed, once studied in depth, this skill in particular is a foundational component of the historical discipline.

It should be noted that the first three skills have been given lower case abbreviations because they are building block skills in the social studies classroom. The other four skills use these foundational systems of analysis in compounding ways and will be given with upper case abbreviations due to their complexity.

How the Skill Works

While continuities over time, exhibited as patterns, are fairly straightforward, there are actually three components associated with the analysis of changes over time: contextual circumstances present before a development, a precipitating factor or a series of factors leading to a development, and characteristics that then exist after the development changed circumstances. Originating conditions are contextual in nature, such as 18th century domestic manufacturing. This is necessary in presentation because the context is used to compare "before" to "after" regarding a change. Next in the analysis are precipitating factors of a development which can be either immediate turning points, such as the invention of the cotton gin, or gradual in nature, such as the Industrial Revolution. The development itself is isolated as the change, such as increased mass production, and is always indicated with an action verb, in this case "increased". Finally, the conditions that present once the change has been affected, offer a new context which when compared to the conditions "before", prove a change happened. In this instance, a prevalence of factory-based manufacturing at the end of the 19th century is juxtaposed to the pre-Industrial Revolution conditions to illustrate the change due to mass production. Once continuities and changes are analyzed over a given period of time, the skill is completed when a concluding sentence is produced. To see how this skill is broken down and organized into its component parts, review the chart below:

"Before": *contextual circumstances present before a development*	**"Factor(s) and Development"**: *a precipitating factor or a series of them leading to a development*	**"After"**: *characteristics that then exist after the development changed circumstances*
18th century domestic manufacturing	Industrial Revolution *increased* mass production	19th century factory-based manufacturing

Teaching changes over time can be challenging because there is a disguised incorporation of causal relationships to explain precipitating factors that led to the development. However, this step is crucial to explaining the nuance behind the change. When expressed in a causal relationship, the precipitating factors are the *cause*, the *how* indicated by an action verb is the factors' influence on the circumstance, and the development is the *effect*. In the example of the Industrial Revolution used in the table above, the *cause* could be technological advancements in manufacturing, the *how* would then be the decreased cost in the production of goods, and the *effect* would be increased mass production. For a review of the component parts of causal relationships, see Chapter 4. When working with students on enhancing their ability to perform analysis with continuities and changes over time, it will be important to highlight this embedded causal relationship.

Teaching the Students

As is good practice when introducing the skill to students, the arduous process of how this skill works is best seen though an example. Consider a scenario wherein a woman looks back on her year and realizes that over the course of the year she started spending more money as she bought a new car and started going to more expensive restaurants. She recognizes her life has changed for the better. She begins to consider why her standard of living has improved and whether her life has changed a lot or a little. First, the woman recognizes that there was a turning point where she received a sizable raise at work after her annual review. However, she knows this was precipitated by a movement to a new team that she liked a lot better which inspired her to work harder. Yet not everything has changed in her life, she recognizes after reflecting on the changes since she still lives in the same apartment and cannot yet afford to go on a long-planned trip to Italy.

Given the scenario, the woman's year can be audited for the varied parts of the change and continuity skill that can be delineated into a graphic organizer as seen on the next page. Utilize the prompt: *"What changes or continuities occurred over time because of the woman's larger income?"* The woman was inspired to reflect on the year after her raise occurred based on her perception of change over time. This required more in-depth analysis, and only later did she admit some continuities after reflection, which could be inserted into the "continuity" section. Changes require more in-depth analysis, even though she instinctively processed them first, by separating the patterns in her life into a "before", a "development," and an "after", and only then observing the continuities in isolation from those changes. By identifying these four groupings, the woman is completing the first step in the analysis process.

Before old car, fast food	Factor(s) and Development new team *led to* raise	After new car, nice restaurants
Continuity Same apartment, no vacation		

Sentence stems for this part of the process applied to this scenario would be as follows:

Stem	Example	Inherent Factors
Before (Development), ...	*Before the raise, the woman drove an old car and ate fast food.*	Pre-existing conditions or context (See Chapter 6: c/x)
(Precipitating factors leading to Development)...	*The woman was moved to a new team which got her a raise because she started working harder with her new friendly colleague.*	Precipitating factor: moved to a new team Turning Point: raise thus Cause: moved to a new team How: started working harder Effect: raise (See Chapter 4: c/e)
After (Development), ...	*After her raise the woman bought a new car and started eating at fancy restaurants.*	Cause: raise How: increased income Effect: increased spending
Yet (Continuity) ...	*Yet, she didn't go on vacation or change her apartment.*	Patterns unaffected by changes

Given that the topic of the prompt is about the woman's larger income, her analysis continues as she identifies the verb to describe the changes that are happening if they are present, the contiguous patterns of life that stayed the same, and the processes in her life that are or are not being affected. These conclusions will likely be some of the most difficult tasks for students to complete as it requires them to form original thoughts rather than just record patterns that they have seen outlined in history. It also requires them to apply causation to an analysis of changes and draw conclusions about continuities. Thus, the following sentence stem should be utilized to outline this process more clearly as this skill is formally introduced. This will provide a scaffold for students to use with this challenging skill:

	Stem	Example	Inherent Factors
Focused on changes	Due to (development), (topic) (verb) in (process).	*Due to her raise, the woman's larger income increased her standard of living.*	<u>Development</u>: raise <u>Topic</u>: larger income <u>Verb</u>: increased <u>Process</u>: standard of living
Focused on continuities	Despite (development), (process) remained the same because (continuity).	*Despite her raise, the woman's standard of living remained the same because she stayed in the same house.*	<u>Development</u>: raise <u>Process</u>: standard of living <u>Continuity</u>: stayed in the same house

Observe how this skill works in a historical example when presented with the prompt: *"How did the French and Indian War change the relationship between English colonies and their mother country of Britain?"* The first step in the process of change and continuity over time is to identify what the development is that is fostering change, the state of the central topic of the prompt before the development and after the development, as well as any continuities.

Before Colonies were allies with England	**Factor(s) and Development** War expenses *increased* English debt	**After** Taxation to pay off the debt without representation increased animosity between the colonies and England
Continuity Colonies dependent on British manufacturing		

The next level of complexity is to flesh out sentence stems for this first step of the process:

Stem	Example	Inherent Factors
Before (Development), ...	*Before the accumulation of war debt, the colonies were allies with Britain in their colonial era.*	Pre-existing conditions or context (See Chapter 6: c/x)
(Precipitating factors leading to Development) ...	*In order to pay for the French and Indian War, England accumulated war debt because the war was so expensive.*	Precipitating factor: French Indian War costs Turning Point: accumulated war debt <u>thus</u> Cause: costs of war How: expensive Effect: debt after war (See Chapter 4: c/e)
After (Development),...	*After gathering war debt, England increased taxes with only virtual representation for colonies which increased tension and animosity between England and her colonies.*	Cause: war debt How: taxed without representation Effect: animosity
Yet (Continuity)...	*Yet, colonies remained dependent on Britain to manufacture finished products from their raw materials.*	Patterns unaffected by changes

Once the students have a mastered understanding of the French and Indian War as a turning point, the following sentence stem could still be utilized to build concluding sentences:

	Stem	Example	Inherent Factors
Focused on changes	Due to (development), (topic) (verb) in (process).	*Due to the war debts accumulated from the French and Indian War, the relationship between Britain and her colonies experienced increased animosity.*	<u>Development</u>: war debts <u>Topic</u>: relationship between England and her colonies <u>Verb</u>: increased <u>Process</u>: animosity
Focused on continuities	Despite (development), (process) remained the same because (continuities).	*Despite the fact that there was an increase in animosity due to tax laws passed to cover war debts, the economic relationship between Britain and her colonies remained materially the same because the colonies were dependent on British manufacturing.*	<u>Development</u>: war debts leading to animosity <u>Process</u>: economic relationship <u>Continuities</u>: dependency on manufacturing

A seasoned historian or teacher may instinctively draw conclusions about changes and continuities, not even aware of the multiple steps involved in the cognitive task. Yet students who lack this historical thinking training may find this scaffolding particularly beneficial in isolating the multiple steps required to perform critical thinking analysis. Students find the matching of sentence stem parts to appropriate and relevant information helpful in organizing more complex thinking as matching is a skill they have long since mastered and are more comfortable utilizing. This then allows for prior knowledge to be engaged in new and more complex thinking tasks growing students' abilities to think critically.

A suggested version of an anchor chart for this skill is on the next page:

Change and Continuity Over Time (CCOT)

Student can discern that continuities and changes over time are being assessed and accurately respond by isolating and describing these patterns. Student can differentiate between continuities and changes over time within and across time periods.

Circumstances present before the development	A turning point or a series of factors and *how* it led to a development	Characteristics that exist after the development
Characteristics that stayed the same over a specific period of time or across time periods			

change

Example:
Due to a completed maturation, the apple tree started to produce apples. Despite completed maturation, the apple tree kept growing taller.

continuity

Troubleshooting

Student Misconception 1: Not answering the prompt

One common issue with not only change and continuity, but all of the skills, is that students will provide an answer that, while true and specific, does not specifically answer the prompt. Given the French and Indian War example, students would likely try to focus on the aftermath of the French and Indian War because of the major changes in the Revolutionary era with which they are much more familiar, rather than the events of the war itself.

Prompt: "How did the French and Indian War change the relationship between English colonies and their mother country of Britain?"

Neither of these student responses answers the prompt:
Example 1: Due to the French and Indian War, England started raising taxes.
Example 2: Due to the increase in taxation, the colonies launched a revolution.

In the first example, the student does not identify a development; instead, they substitute the topic of the prompt, which provides no evidence of original thinking in the argument. In addition, it focuses on the changes that happen after the war without any connection to the topic which is the war itself. In the second example, the student identifies an off-topic development and change, one from the next era in history, not from the events that happened during the French and Indian War. Thus, it will be important to remind students when looking at a historical question that they need to focus on what the prompt is asking them. In the previous example any answer needs to respond to what is happening to the *relationship* due to the turning point of the *French and Indian War.*

Student Misconception 2: Not connecting themes across time

In addition, remind students that they need to have a consistent theme or topic from the "before" to the "after" in order to build a coherent argument. Again, in the example provided previously they are focusing on the *relationship* between England and the colonies, so that should be the topic in both the "before" and "after." See the non-example below:

Before	*After*
Colonists identified as British citizens	*Taxation without representation*

This student response might appear to be true at first glance; however, upon reflection the "before" is a comment on the identity relationship between England and her colonies, whereas the "after" is about the political relationship associated with taxation. This student would then struggle to build a coherent argument about the process that is occurring, forced to choose between an identity relationship and a political relationship. It would be virtually impossible for a student to identify and argue *one thing*, i.e., the process, which has changed over time in terms of relationship based on this initial brainstorming. Referring students back to the tools provided by using sentence stem graphic organizing boxes will allow them to ensure parallelism throughout their answer. In addition, providing narrative feedback when students deviate from the theme they have selected will allow them to find where they are losing their train of thought, usually in diagnosing the process part of the changes over time.

Student Misconception 3: Being distracted by the tools

Some students will find the detailed sentence stems more laborious than simply attempting to cover the three major components of change over time and at least one continuity in their responses. If the sentence stems create barriers for students alternative methods can be used so long as all components of the skill are in evidence. An alternative method for students to use in recording their assessments of the information needed to answer the prompt, especially for those who are visual-spatial learners, is the employment of scientific notation. Students can use the Greek symbol "delta" (Δ) to symbolize "change in", a horizontal arrow ($\rightarrow$) to represent continuities, directional arrows to show a decrease or increase ($\uparrow$ or $\downarrow$), and custom pictographs that allow the student to complete their analysis about key characteristics. It is important to emphasize for students that scientific notation is not a simplification or a shortcut to analysis. Scientific notation, or alternative means of symbol use, is simply a different methodology for completing the same steps in the thinking skill as it requires the same analysis of "before - process - after - continuity" in any given circumstance but does provide an alternate means of recording that thinking. For the teacher, utilizing scientific notation can not only introduce this alternative to visual-spatial learners, but also make more efficient the process of in class instruction on change and continuity over time and giving narrative feedback.

Student Misconception 4: Missing a verb

If the student is struggling with analyzing changes, often the component that is missing is identifying the verb to use in describing what changes are happening. A change by definition is an action that has occurred, so students will be unsuccessful in answering a question about change without identifying the process using an action verb. See the example below regarding the French and Indian War as fostering change:

> **Student response without action verb:** *After the French and Indian War the British Parliament taxed without representation to pay off their war debt.*

In the student example above, note that the student appears to be simply providing information they were taught. They have not identified the change that has taken place which would require them to analyze the information and find an action verb to show the change. Instead, the student should say that there was an *increase* in taxation. This then separates the era into "before" the war when the colonies had been taxed without representation with no real opposition and "after" the war where there is opposition, which highlights the increase in taxation as a catalyst for change. Here again, scientific notation can help students remind themselves to indicate an action verb for every change they want to identify. For clarifying increases and decreases, utilize up and down arrows as mentioned to ensure students identify changes using action verbs in their responses.

Student Misconception 5: Lack of prior skill competency

Students are often challenged by the multiple steps required to perform this skill. Students are prone to focus on just the development or the outcome as they tend to overlook the cause-and-effect relationship disguised within a continuity and change analysis. Or students may become hyper focused on what they see as the more obvious of the two characteristics - continuities OR changes (which is akin to their accidental blindness to similarities or differences). Because people tend to be naturally attuned to changes in the environment, it can help for students to focus first on perceived changes in order to clear the mental pallet, allowing for continuities to reveal themselves. When these challenges arise, it is important for the teacher to assess whether or not students have a firm understanding of what is required in performing the previously taught skills. Does the student know how to connect the cause, how, and effect of causation? Does the student know how to compare changes and continuities? These earlier skills are distinct in and of themselves and are inherently required to complete CCOT effectively (see chapter 4 and chapter 5 troubleshooting).

Importance of Change and Continuity over Time

Continuities and changes over time are the foundation of any analysis of historical patterns. Due to the necessary proficiency in other skills, namely those of causation and comparison, this skill is more challenging than the skills previously discussed. With practice students can learn to overcome the challenges of a more detailed analysis of these patterns, allowing them to appreciate social studies in new ways. When internalized, college students will be able to effectively see patterns in challenging courses and adjust their performance based on their analysis of changes over time in feedback from their professors. Later in life, adults appreciate continuities in relationships, often highlighting the changes that might be needed for continued personal growth. The end goal is for students to be able to transfer this ability to assess patterns of continuity and change over time throughout their daily lives as adults, empowering them to analyze their own personal budgets, relationships and contributions to society.

Social Studies Examples by Subject

In the examples over the next few pages, the various sentence stems, conclusion sentences, and some variations therein are utilized to form a coherent paragraph fully answering each change and continuity question.

World Geography prompt:

"How has the Sahara Desert changed and stayed the same over time?"

Change	Before True desert size mostly very top of North Africa	Factor(s) and Development Over-farming beginning about 50 years ago and goat herding *increased* desertification	After Expansion of the Sahara
Continuity	Continued issue of water scarcity for the people living there		
Student Response	*Due to over-farming and the increased herding of goats, the Sahara Desert has grown significantly in size. Before over-farming and increased goat herding, the true size of the Sahara Desert was just over 3 million square miles in the 1920s. However, over-farming has dried out adjacent Sahel land and grazing goats have ripped out the roots of plants leading to desertification. After over-farming and increased goat herding, the Sahara has grown by 10% since studies started in the 1920s. Yet the people living in and around the Sahara struggle with water scarcity, regardless of the size of the desert.*		

World History prompt:

"How was the Yalta Conference a turning point for Germany?"

Change	Before Germany united Hitler reigned	Factor(s) and Development Yalta Conference leaders *split* control of Germany	After Lost the war Allied leaders artificially divided Germany
Continuity	Significant role in Cold War		
Student Response	*Although Germany would continue to play an integral role in rising tensions throughout the Cold War, decisions made by Allied Leaders at the Yalta Conference led to Germany's division which would compromise the unity once experienced by German people. Before the Yalta Conference, Germany was one united state as they had been during Hitler's nationalistic reign in World War II. At the Yalta conference, the soon to be victorious Allied leaders aimed to split control of the country in order to rebuild Germany. In the end, the Yalta Conference divided Germany into four distinct administrative zones controlled by England, France, the United States, and the Soviet Union which persisted until the end of the Cold War. Despite the Yalta Conference dividing Germany geographically into zones, the German people and the German state continued to play a major ideological role in the escalating Cold War.*		

<u>United States History prompt</u>:

"How did the Continental Army's international alliances change throughout the American Revolution?"

Change	Before No alliances with other countries Natives align with Britain	Factor(s) and Development Victory at Saratoga *increased* prestige internationally	After French Alliance provided increased naval and army power during the war Formed permanent alliance with France
Continuity	Broken alliance with Britain since they were revolting		
Student Response	*Due to the victory at the Battle of Saratoga, the Continental Army was able to secure the recognition and support of the French government for the remainder of the American Revolution. Before the Battle of Saratoga, the revolting colonists had no alliances with any other country and many Native Americans had chosen to align with the British. However, the victory at Saratoga proved to foreign countries that the Continental Army would be capable of victory if provided additional military and financial assistance. After Saratoga, the colonies and France signed a Treaty of Alliance in 1778 which provided French naval and army power to the colonists, eventually securing victory in the war. Understandably, the Continental Army continued to maintain a broken alliance with Britain throughout the war since they were revolting against them.*		

Government prompt:

"How have amendments made to the Constitution altered or maintained the original document?"

Change	Before Constitution in original form	Factor(s) and Development Bill of Rights *added* human rights 16th, 19th, 26th amendments *granted* suffrage	After Liberties enshrined Greater equality
Continuity	Powers of branches not materially altered Implied and inherent powers Growth of bureaucracy		
Student Response	*Despite 27 different amendments to the Constitution which have secured civil liberties and provided greater equality, the powers each branch of the United States government wields have not been significantly changed by the amendments to the Constitution. The Bill of Rights secured liberties for individual Americans and the 15th, 19th, and 26th amendments marked a change by increasing suffrage. However, the powers inherent and listed in Articles I, II, and III have rarely been altered and have seen little to no significant change to the original document. Although powers associated with the branches have seen a continued expansion of bureaucracy and continuous expanded interpretations of inherent and implied powers of each branch, the original document of the Constitution has not been altered by amendments to incorporate these changes. Therefore, there has been greater continuity in the original document than changes made by what the amendments might suggest.*		

Economics prompt:

"If a new automobile maker enters the market, what changes would an economist expect to see in the automobile market?"

Change	Before Auto market is stable	Factor(s) and Development New auto maker enters market meaning supply *increases*, so prices fall	After Quantity demanded increases
Continuity	Buyers' income doesn't change		
Student Response	*Before a new supplier enters the market, supply of automobiles originates at an equilibrium price of $10,000 and a quantity demanded of 100 automobiles. Due to an increase in the number of sellers in the market, the market for automobiles will see an increase in supply of automobiles. Therefore, the price falls which triggers a greater quantity demanded. So that, after a new supplier enters the market, supply of automobiles increases to create a new equilibrium price of $9,000 and an increase in quantity demanded to 110 automobiles. Therefore, even though buyer's income remains constant, an increase in the number of sellers in the market will lead to a decrease in the price of automobiles and the market will experience an increase in the quantity demanded of automobiles.*		

Psychology prompt:

"How has the study of Learning changed and stayed the same over time?"

Change	Before Philosophical Pre-Scientific Psychology	Factor(s) and Development Introduction of experimental psychology *increased* use of the scientific method	After Behaviorism
Continuity	Observing behavior		
Student Response	*Due to the introduction of experimental psychology, the study of Learning became more scientific. The early philosophers of psychology focused on studying the mind in order to explain behavior, such as Rene Descartes and John Locke. However, during the Industrial Revolution, the introduction of experimental psychology by Wilhelm Wundt changed the study of behavior to one utilizing the scientific method. After this change, psychologists such as Ivan Pavlov and John Watson pioneered Behaviorism as the scientific study of observable behavior. Yet, throughout the history of the discipline, psychologists continued to observe behavior in order to draw their conclusions.*		

Change and Continuity over Time (CCOT) Reflection

At this point, readers may be feeling overwhelmed and yet excited to see these skills in action. It is important to be patient and forgiving as more complex skills, such as CCOT, are implemented, misinterpreted, and eventually mastered. Do not be afraid to try using CCOT, knowing that with time and reflection instructors and students will become more proficient. Here are some metacognitive questions to get started with reflection:

1. How has your understanding of change and continuity over time (CCOT) been altered after reading this chapter?

2. What do you think your students' reaction will be to these new revelations about all the previous skills required to analyze changes and continuities?

3. Where do you anticipate your students having the most misunderstandings and what scaffolding will they need when introduced to the skill?

4. What steps do you need to take to increase your confidence in generating and grading CCOT prompts?

5. How will you implement the CCOT skill in a lesson in your classroom?

Chapter 8:

Interpretation (I)

Skill Overview

Interpretation is a vital skill for students to learn because it teaches them how to objectively analyze what creates people's opinions about topics. Beyond listing relevant facts about an author or person, interpretation asks students to explain "why *this* person would feel *this* way about *this* topic." After finding contributing factors to a particular subject's point of view, students must abstract why the factors they chose are significant to that person's perspective. Then, students relate how those factors are significant to a particular topic at hand and the resulting point of view.

How To

Step 1: Identify 2-3 contributing factors that influence point of view (like CORNPEG)

Step 2: Abstraction of the factors' significance

Step 3: Explain how those highlighted factors and abstraction are significant to the topic at hand

Graphic Organizer

Step 1: Relevant CORNPEG Factors	Step 2: Abstraction of 2-3 Factors	Step 3: Significance to Topic

Sentence Stems

"As (factors), (person) believes/feels (opinion) about (topic) because (significance)."

Example

A single mother of two children who happen to share a birthday, needs to buy a birthday cake. As a mother, she wants to minimize sibling rivalry and ensure each child feels equally and uniquely celebrated so she buys two cakes. Yet, as a single parent, she has a finite budget with little room for extra expenditures. Therefore, she will likely feel anxiety about these conflicting pressures and will not enjoy the cakes and party as much as her children.

Introduction to Interpretation

Before secondary education, students have repeatedly been asked to identify the author of a source, perhaps decide if the source is biased or valid, and may have been introduced to identifying the context of a source. Yet, these activities do not actively employ the disciplinary skill that is so vital to historical study: analyzing the ways in which factors of a source's authorship contribute to understanding and utilizing a source. The skill of interpretation can be utilized not only for document analysis, but with each person, nation, and perspective discussed in social studies. History is the study of people and their choices in the past, and thus the interpretation skill is vital to analysis in the discipline. In fact, the interpretation skill can be used to explain behavior, choices, reactions, and even events. Interpretation allows for valuable analysis in multiple contexts and across many tasks in the social studies classroom. Explaining how valuable the skill is allows students to become more comfortable with transferring this skill and utilizing it at will in a variety of contexts, including beyond the classroom. Ultimately educators hope that the transferability of what they teach in the classroom will build their students into better people and more compassionate citizens as well as valuable contributors to their communities. Purposeful instruction in interpretation will teach students to become more empathetic and open-minded individuals because they are systematically practicing viewing world events from other peoples' points of view in a meaningful way.

How the Skill Works

For average teenagers, it is often difficult to put themselves in someone else's shoes in order to figure out "why *this* person would feel *this* way about *this* topic." This is because interpreting requires a level of empathy that is still developing in adolescence. Adolescents in general have a limited frame of reference when it comes to characteristics associated with socio-economic classes other than their own, the implications of being trained for any one occupation, the various conclusions one can draw about biases associated with conflicting political perspectives, and more. Their context for each of these personality characteristics is limited to their own personal real-world experience and thus, often needs to be supplemented with direct instruction.

Consider a scenario where a mother is frustrated with her son who, after being asked repeatedly to fulfill a responsibility, has still neglected to do so. The mother shouts to the son: "I asked you to clean your room five times, what is wrong with you? Do it now!" The teenager's reaction to this exclamation will likely be anger or indignation and he may even decide not to clean his room to spite her. Yet, if the teen is able to set aside his instinctual adverse reaction and consider the point of view, or perspective, of his mother, he may begin to understand why she is yelling. The teen could instead ask himself, "Why does my mom feel so strongly about my bedroom being clean?"

As a *parent*, there may be a certain level of respect the mother expects to receive when directions are given. As a *provider*, she might feel taken advantage of when material goods she paid for are not taken care of by him. As a *woman*, she may feel frustrated that the next escalation might include the lines "Wait until your father gets home!", indicating that some other gender or parent has greater power. Considering his mother had already worked a full day as an *employee*, she is likely very tired. Based on his analysis of all these factors, cleaning his room does not seem to be such a big task to ask of him given her perspective. He decides it makes sense now why she's angry, so he complies. Here the son has fully completed the interpretation skill in order to understand why his mother feels so angry about him not cleaning his room, which ultimately alters his behavior and improves his practice of empathizing with others.

In essence, interpretation is the analysis of the contributing factors to various points of view; but this is a complex activity. To perform the skill of interpreting a point of view, there needs to be a systemic mechanism for breaking down those contributing factors to make this complex task more manageable as it is being learned. In this way, interpretation is much more than simply identifying an author, date, or context; it is explaining how multiple factors may influence the opinion of the person being analyzed and their responses to the topic at hand.

How to Track Progress

"When I first implemented the skills system, the students were not totally comfortable tracking progress with their skills because they were so used to receiving feedback on how well they learned the content. So, I implemented a portfolio system, as many teachers do, and had the students track their feedback on each of the skills as they got work back. Each student keeps a binder in my classroom divided into the skills, eras of history, type of task, or quarters of the year so that nothing will get lost. The students track their proficiency in the front of the binder on each skill as they get work so that they can watch skill development over time. I also allow students to redo work based on my narrative feedback in my class as additional refinement of skills and evidence of mastery, while also helping the students practice reflecting on growth. This portfolio system helps them to decide which skills they need to improve, which tasks to redo, and keeps track of completed work so they don't throw it away. This system facilitates the ability to observe long term patterns of improvement encouraging perseverance. This can also easily be done digitally using a tracking template and an online portfolio system."

– Toms

Teaching the Students

After introducing a topic and a person to analyze, step one of interpretation is to identify two or three contributing factors or personal characteristics that may have influenced the person, or at least informed his point of view. The most relevant characteristics tend to be topic-dependent; that is, their relevancy is uniquely tied to the context of a topic. To help students organize relevance of characteristics use CORNPEG which is common acronym to support students in their exploration of point of view. CORNPEG stands for:

Class
Occupation
Religion
Nationality
Political perspective
Ethnicity
Gender

However, contributing factors to point of view are not limited to this brief list, they could also include the person's age, education, family situation, previous experience, and other topic-dependent factors. Once the students have applied CORNPEG to a perspective, they must then decide which two to three factors likely have most influenced the point of view of the author.

In the earliest attempts at this skill, students will need to identify many factors to consider in order to find the most relevant ones that establish significance in point of view. It is important to note that students will rarely need to have answers to every letter of the acronym and may indeed not even have access to all characteristic information. Reminding students of this will help them manage the time committed to reflecting on any one perspective's background information. In addition, the class lesson on a particular person may have already provided the two or three salient characteristics which ought to be referenced. Yet providing this scaffolding will help students by offering them guidance in the practice of interpretation which will add confidence to their practice of this skill. Previously in academics students have likely had practice only *identifying* information about authors, their opinions, and the source itself. However, that level of practice is limited to Lower Bloom's, where only the demonstration of understanding and application levels of thinking are utilized. Additional *analysis* is required in order to perform the abstract thinking required for true interpretation to occur.

Step two includes an abstraction of the implications of the two to three salient characteristics selected about the speaker or author. In essence, the students must answer the question "so what?" The students need to identify the implications of the characteristics in the person or groups' overall identity and interactions. For example, when discussing a letter from the Pope to Genghis Khan, students might identify as salient characteristics that his religion is Catholic and his occupation is the Pope. But the implications, which often go overlooked until a refined practicing of this skill is taught, is that as head of the Catholic church, he has specific responsibilities to advocate for Christians worldwide and that he acts as a representative and leader of the faith. The abstraction of these factors could suggest that not only would Christians respect his guidance, but also that he has a responsibility to speak on behalf of his adherents. Note that this step does not yet apply the information to the topic; it focuses instead on general implications of a person's standing in society, experience, emotions, etc.

Step three requires the students to utilize the factors *and* abstractions they identified and explain how they are significant to the topic. In this step, using the above referenced example of the Pope writing a letter to Genghis Khan, one can use the implications of the Catholic Pope's responsibilities to and position in the Christian church to explain why he might reach out to the leader of a foreign and violent population with whom the church would not have otherwise interacted. When he wrote the letter he advocated for his followers and tried to influence a reduction of violence against them. Interpretation, when executed thoroughly, allows students to suggest motivations for historical figures' actions in history. This last step is the one where students are finally performing truly critical thinking about point of view. Students are required to provide the significance of the abstraction as it relates to a topic in order to show they have successfully performed the skill of interpretation. In essence, the student should be able to communicate: "why *this* person feels *this* way about *this* topic".

The table on the next page applies the interpretation skill to the topic of the Treaty of Versailles and the point of view of Adolf Hitler. Note that some CORNPEG characteristics were deemed less relevant, so the abstraction step was not recorded. Only four characteristics are focused on in this analysis: occupation, nationality, political perspective, and ethnicity. The abstraction created from those four would be the focus of the suggestions from the student regarding Hitler's perspective on the Treaty of Versailles.

CORNPEG: Possible factors or characteristics	Step 1: Factors applied to <u>Adolf Hitler</u>	Step 2: Abstraction about factor: Why does this matter?	Step 3: Factor and abstraction's significance to the topic: <u>Treaty of Versailles</u>
Class: To what socio-economic class does this person belong?	Less relevant		All citizens were impacted by hyperinflation, so this characteristic is less relevant
Occupation: What did this person do for a living?	Nazi party leader	In a position where people will listen to him	Promoted a solution to resentment about imposed conditions of treaty
Religion: What values did this person hold from their religious beliefs?	Less relevant		Since religious activity was minimized during the Nazi regime, this is a less relevant characteristic
Nationality: To what nation does this person belong?	German	Very patriotic, angry over treaty	This particular category was the pivotal characteristic used to bolster Nazi party initiatives as responses to the treaty
Political perspective: What opinions do they hold based on their political ideology?	National Socialist Party	Fascist supporter of big government	The party fueled a unification against the treaty and helped form responses to it
Ethnicity: What ethnic community memberships does this person possess?	White, Anglo-Saxon, Protestant	WASP ethnocentrism	This characteristic informed the superiority complex of the Nazi party
Gender: What role does gender play?	Less relevant		Less relevant as both sexes were affected by the treaty equally

While the CORNPEG chart as a handout is a valuable tool for students to use with specific activities around a predetermined topic, it is also helpful to have an anchor chart in the classroom that reminds students of the skill and the tools associated with its use such as the one below:

Interpretation (I)

Student can discern that interpretation is being assessed, and can isolate contributing factors to various points of view.

C lass
O ccupation
R eligion
N ationality
P olitical view
E thnicity
G ender
And more...

"Why does *this* person feel *this* way about *this* topic?"

Example: What explains John Doe's reaction to changes in the stock market?

Step 1:
C - Middle
O - Farmer
R - Baptist
N - American
P - Republican
E - Caucasian
G - Male

Step 2:
Not affluent, must plan for retirement savings

Knows about fluctuations in crop prices

Concerned about free market economic policies

Step 3: As a Republican middle class farmer, John Doe fears fluctuation of the stock market in commodity price changes because he wants to ensure he maximizes crop sales and retirement savings based on free market trends.

One way to scaffold for lower performing students is to ask them to focus on analyzing just one CORNPEG factor more thoroughly, rather than implement two or three at a time. Analyzing two or three factors provides nuance to an argument; however, it may overload the underperformer. Instead, ask them to CORNPEG the perspective and then just pick one factor to abstract and provide significance for so that it is easier to diagnose where the student struggles most. This level of *depth* in analysis is just as valuable in terms of abstract thinking as the more nuanced *breadth* of analysis using multiple factors. It should be noted that interpretation is so reliant upon factors that sentence stems are not as useful to this skill. However, if one is required the following will suffice:

"*As* (factors), (person) *believes/feels* (opinion) *about* (topic) *because* (significance)." Yet, interpretation can be used in a myriad of situations and is not only applicable for simple discussion or arbitrary analysis. In fact, one of its most common uses in social studies classrooms is for document analysis.

Document Analysis with Interpretation and Contextualization

One of the cornerstone skills of the social studies discipline is the ability to analyze a primary or secondary source. In contemporary curriculum, there is a focus on the Document Based Question (DBQ) which essentially expects students to utilize and cite sources to support a thesis in an essay. After instruction on reading and understanding the content of the source, students should be expected to analyze the source leveraging their historical thinking skills. An acronym students can utilize for this Upper Bloom's analysis is CAP. CAP stands for:

Context
Audience/purpose
Point of view

Using this acronym, the students will be expected to use the contextualization skill for context and the interpretation skill to analyze point of view. The audience portion asks the students to identify what the purpose of the author was in addressing an intended audience. Analyzing the Context, Audience, and Point of View of a document will generate complexity in document interpretation.

All three steps ask the students to go beyond *identifying* or summarizing information about the document, and instead ask the students to critically *analyze* the document. For contextualization, students must identify the era in which the document originated, generating both big themes and details about the context, and abstract significance to the prompt or the argument. In regard to the audience, students must identify and connect the audience and purpose of the document and then abstract significance to the prompt or the argument. Finally, for point of view, students must complete the interpretation skill by identifying factors about the author of the document and then, after abstraction, connect the author's feelings or opinions to the prompt or argument. To see the CAP process in action, review the prompt and table of analysis on the next page:

Prompt: How does the Declaration of Independence reflect intellectual ideals?

Source: Excerpt from the "Declaration of Independence", adopted by the Second Continental Congress on July 4, 1776

"We hold these truths to be self-evident, that all men are created equal, that they are endowed by their Creator with certain unalienable Rights, that among these are Life, Liberty and the pursuit of Happiness.--That to secure these rights, Governments are instituted among Men, deriving their just powers from the consent of the governed, --That whenever any Form of Government becomes destructive of these ends, it is the Right of the People to alter or to abolish it, and to institute new Government, laying its foundation on such principles and organizing its powers in such form, as to them shall seem most likely to effect their Safety and Happiness."

CAP	Example	Abstraction	Significance
Context: when and where was the document written?	In the British colonies of North America after Lexington and Concord in the mid-1770s	Thomas Paine's *Common Sense* (detail) and Enlightenment thinking (big theme) prevalent in this era and location	The recent military conflict with the British and Enlightenment thinking drove the founders to draft this radical missive of departure from Britain
Audience: to whom is the document addressed and for what purpose?	To King George and the rest of the world to officially submit grievances	Advertised to world that colonies were no longer interested in resolving issues with mother country	An effort was being made to enlist support for independence through acknowledgement of sovereignty by other sovereign nations, if not Britain
Point of View: what factors influence the author's perspective about the topic?	Author: Thomas Jefferson and other similar men* C aristocratic O landowner N British P Patriot *factors less related to the Declaration of Independence have been omitted	Aristocratic landowners* invested in ensuring freedom for their business choices would expect equal treatment under law as wealthy contributing members of society. *In the abstraction pick 2 to 3 relevant topics to address.	Jefferson and other wealthy founding fathers were economically invested in establishing an autonomous nation because they were aristocratic landowners. The language of equality in the Declaration is a manifestation of this expectation.

While this skill is often employed for text excerpts from historical documents, it cannot be ignored that the same skill is utilized in assessment of visual data as well. This includes charts, maps, graphs, political cartoons, artwork, and any other documents that require interpretation. Students can leverage CAP to critically analyze any source, as the context, audience, and point of view are consistently useful in informing analysis. Not every element of the acronym CAP will be equally relevant to every source. For example, in data sets, context is often going to be the most critical component in interpretation, but not always. Using CAP for document analysis requires direct instruction and extensive modeling given the variety of uses for which it will be endlessly employed.

Troubleshooting

Student Misconception 1: Inaccurately focused on validity or reliability

Interpretation may be stunted if a student decides that the author of the source is biased or wrong, thus in their mind invalidating the source and dismissing its usefulness. For example, if a student isolates the point of view of an author as being racist, they may conclude that the source isn't reliable due to the author's bias. They may then dismiss its reliability and believe they have completed interpretation. In reality, a racist point of view can still be leveraged to analyze a particularly racist era. Distinguish for students that while bias must be taken into account during interpretation, opinions are not less valuable just because they are informed by characteristics or factors of the author. In fact, that is the essence of the skill. Using CORNPEG to isolate which characteristics of the author to focus on can help resolve these issues by highlighting factors that give the author credibility despite opinions with which the student may disagree. In addition, remind the students that they do not need to agree with a point of view in order to utilize it. For example, students can convince themselves that if they sympathize with American Gilded Age Robber Barons that they are then in agreement with the exploitation of the mid-19th century urban poor. Educators and historians know this is not the case. Discuss with the students that mastering interpretation will help them learn how to entertain a point of view without agreeing with it.

Analyzing for validity and reliability is in some ways critical to and the purpose of analysis, but it should not be used to discount a source or perspective. Thus, it may be helpful to highlight for students the increased potential for validity and reliability of secondary sources as they have the benefit of hindsight and a more objective view on historical situations and consequences, particularly when analyzing documents. Conversely, most primary sources, being situated in their time, will all have inherent bias which may call into question the validity of the opinions in the document, but should not negate the validity of the application of the document in the student's analysis.

Student Misconception 2: Focus on irrelevant factors

Focusing on less relevant characteristics of the speaker is counterproductive to efficient and relevant analysis. For example, when given a socio-economic context, if a student focuses on an author's religion they are focusing on a less relevant factor. Class or occupation would be more efficiently and effectively useful in explaining "why *this* person feels *this* way about *this* topic". Direct instruction on connecting theme and context to a point of view, as is a factor in many skills, will help students learn to focus on answering a prompt directly rather than circumventing it.

Student Misconception 3: Misinterpreting the source

When interpretation is being utilized to analyze a primary or secondary source, additional student misconceptions arise. Misinterpreting the speaker's tone, misunderstanding the intended audience of a source, and a host of other points of confusion are rampant when it comes to practicing the skill of interpretation with documents. Short excerpts from historical documents offer an opportunity for students to practice understanding the source itself before historical analysis begins. Modeling analysis of author's tone, word choice, vocabulary, as well as surmising purpose can all be useful in overcoming this challenge. Instruction on chunking the source to create summaries as building blocks to understanding can be utilized at the start or end of any class period, or even as a transitional activity as the practice of this skill does takes minimal time when employing only one source.

Importance of Interpretation

Upon reflection, the skill of interpretation, like the other advanced skills, encompasses multiple skills. Interpretation includes primarily causation (Chapter 4) when considering the factors (cause) influence (process) on the significance (effect). While interpretation can be introduced early on, to be mastered, interpretation will take considerable amounts of practice as the skill of causation is adapted and diversified to analyzing perspectives of people and groups. In addition, comparison (Chapter 5) and contextualization (Chapter 6) are also both involved in the process of evaluating factors for relevance, making this thinking process, like change and continuity over time (Chapter 7), one of the most challenging for students of the social studies disciplines. While both continuity and change over time as well as interpretation skills can be deceptive in their complexity, students can indeed practice them at various levels of success while continuing to work toward proficiency and eventually mastery of these abstract thinking skills.

In order for students to be able to appreciate alternative points of view, they have to have some exposure to analysis of different perspectives. Interpretation allows students to enhance their ability to empathize with or at least understand different historical perspectives in order to master the skill. Yet, this skill is exceptionally valuable as a transfer goal in their everyday adult lives as they struggle with coworkers, life partners, and influential peers in their communities. The ability to appreciate an alternative point of view is what allows for compromises to be made, marriages to be reconciled, and wars to be averted. The social studies classroom is a valuable laboratory for experimenting with this skill in order to employ it in the real world throughout one's lifetime.

Social Studies Examples by Subject

World Geography topic: Incan Society on the Andes Mountains

Step 1: Select relevant CORNPEG Factors	Step 2: Abstraction of 2-3 Factors	Step 3: Significance to Topic
Incan Society R - polytheistic animists E - Indigenous Americans	The Incas were polytheistic animists who believed that everything in nature has a spirit and some elements of the environment are gods. They believed that the gods resided in a heaven above them.	**Student Response:** *The Incas lived in the Andes Mountains, and so they believed that the higher into the mountains they went the closer they were to their gods. Instead of building pyramids, the Incas felt the Andes mountains as landforms were intrinsic to their religious experience.*

World History topic: Stalin on Hitler's Invasion of Poland

Step 1: Select relevant CORNPEG Factors	Step 2: Abstraction of 2-3 Factors	Step 3: Significance to Topic
Josef Stalin O - Leader of Russia N - Russian P - Communist	As the leader of his country, communist Stalin would believe other powerful leaders would honor his position by upholding agreements	**Student Response:** *Stalin would shift his allegiance and ally with FDR and Churchill in WWII after he was betrayed in his pact with Hitler by Germany's invasion of Poland*

United States History topic: Colonial Loyalists on The American Revolution

Step 1: Select relevant CORNPEG Factors	Step 2: Abstraction of 2-3 Factors	Step 3: Significance to Topic
Colonial Loyalists O - often merchants P - Tories Other factor: Region - often East Coast	The New England wealthy merchants in port cities were very economically tied to the dependent trade system with Britain. Loyal Tories were also given many positions of power in the colonies and thus benefit from their crown designated roles.	**Student Response:** *The colonial Loyalists were usually economically and politically invested in perpetuating the status quo in the colonies because they were profiting from the dependent relationship with Britain, thus they were inclined to oppose the Revolution.*

Government topic: Chief Justice John Marshall on Marbury v. Madison

Step 1: Select relevant CORNPEG Factors	Step 2: Abstraction of 2-3 Factors	Step 3: Significance to Topic
Chief Justice John Marshall C - Upper class O - Supreme Court Justice P - Federalist	As a Federalist, Marshall would believe in a strong central government, and in fulfilling his role on the Supreme Court, would advocate for expansion of federal powers	**Student Response:** *As a Federalist, Chief Justice Marshall secured the power of Judicial Review for the Supreme Court by determining constitutionality of congressional laws and executive actions ensuring the strengthening of the courts at the Federal level.*

Economics topic: President Ronald Reagan on Reaganomics

Step 1: Select relevant CORNPEG Factors	Step 2: Abstraction of 2-3 Factors	Step 3: Significance to Topic
President Ronald Reagan O-President P-Republican	Republican President Reagan consulted economic advisors who were pro-business to determine how to recover from what he saw as the democratically created stagflation of the 1970s	**Student Response:** *In supporting supply-side theory, Reagan's pro-business republican perspective informed his choice of economic advisors who would create an economic system to benefit producers: Reaganomics.*

Psychology topic: Freudian Psychoanalysts on Learned Helplessness

Step 1: Select relevant CORNPEG Factors	Step 2: Abstraction of 2-3 Factors	Step 3: Significance to Topic
Freudian Psychoanalysts O – psychologist Other factors: Beliefs - paternalistic Training - Freudian	Psychoanalytic psychologists believe that unconscious motives and experiences in early childhood impact personality and behavior. Freud believed that women were inferior to men.	**Student Response:** *Freudian Psychoanalysts would think that women are more susceptible to learned helplessness due to their gender and the vulnerability of their ego which developed in childhood.*

Interpretation (I) Reflection

Here are some metacognitive questions to get started with reflection:

1. How has your understanding of interpretation and points of view changed after reading this chapter?

2. How can students benefit from a proficiency in interpretation in their personal lives outside of school?

3. What do you think your students' reaction will be to these new revelations about points of view?

4. Where do you anticipate your students having the most misunderstandings and what scaffolding will they need when introduced to the skill?

5. What steps do you need to take to increase your confidence in generating and grading interpretation prompts?

6. How will you implement the interpretation skill in a lesson in your classroom?

Chapter 9:

Evaluation (E)

Skill Overview
Evaluation is not as complex to explain as other skills but is arguably one of the most difficult to reliably master. In its simplest form, evaluation is weighing information and choosing a conclusion. However, the weighing information step requires students to categorize and compare information, amongst other skills. Information can be categorized into dichotomous, thematic, time-bound, or attribute structures. Then, students must executively choose a conclusion based on their analysis, resulting in either yes, no, or sometimes as a product of their evaluation. Particularly if there is no obvious choice, this step can prove difficult.

How To
Step 1: Weigh evidence through comparison and categorization
Step 2: Rank significance of each piece of evidence
Step 3: Choose conclusion based on evidence analyzed (yes, no, or sometimes)

Graphic Organizer

Characteristic 1:	Characteristic 2:	Characteristic 3:
Choice:		

Sentence Stems
Difficult to use sentence stems because evaluation is prompt specific but offering the three options for a specific prompt might be helpful:

Yes, A is better than B. - or -

No, A is not better than B. - or -

A can be better than B given the right conditions.

Example
Vanilla cake is the better cake to use for large gatherings. This is due to the fact that while chocolate may be somewhat popular, there are less people inclined to be opposed to vanilla as it is the more subtle flavor, it doesn't make teeth brown when eaten, and if any falls from the large number of people eating it, it is easier to clean up.

Introduction to Evaluation

The skill of evaluation is very commonly used in education, but it is not often required to be performed at a high enough level to be considered critical thinking. When studied metacognitively, students are actually practicing basic evaluation all the time. At its heart, evaluation is analyzing alternative criteria to determine a conclusion about a topic, in other words weighing information and choosing a conclusion. At first glance, evaluation can be refreshingly familiar after looking at so many complex skills in previous chapters. However, evaluation is one step higher on Bloom's Taxonomy than analysis. Once the metacognition is taught, students should recognize that making a hard decision in their personal lives is more difficult than simply analyzing the consequences of each choice. For example, a student might need to decide whether to stay in an on-level class or to take an AP Social Studies course. The student can easily practice some basic analysis as she makes a pros and cons list of each option. On her list she could consider the workload of each class, the effect on her grade point average, and which classes her friends are going to be taking. Yet despite the beautifully organized list, this student will still struggle to make a final decision because executive functions are only just forming in adolescence. Deciding what shoes to wear that morning had been easy enough, but choices with multiple valid outcomes will prove more difficult. Students need practice making hard choices, and evaluation in social studies provides this practice.

How the Skill Works

The end result of the evaluation skill is the student's ability to make a decision and execute that decision, based on an analysis and assessment of varied information. Multiple research studies summarized by Silver, Strong, and Perini (2007), indicate that practicing evaluation helps students learn information, conceptualize at higher levels, and develop lifelong decision-making skills. For this reason, evaluation is not only flexible, but also a necessary and effective teaching component in successful skills-based classrooms.

In evaluation there are inherently two steps involved: weighing and choosing. The first step in the evaluation process is to weigh factors against each other through analysis. In this way actively evaluating is dependent on having mastered the previous skills introduced and discussed. Most often students will compare factors for their evaluation by categorizing them. There are four types of systematic categorization that are seen in evaluation: dichotomous, thematic, time bound, and attribute based.

Dichotomous weighing may ask students to evaluate in terms of better versus worse, yes versus no, good versus bad, or more versus less. However, multifaceted weighing may require a ranking of categories beyond a two-dimensional scope. These then could be organized by theme, time period, or another attribute. Thematic categorizing could be based on topics such as those included in SPICE. Time bound categorizing could focus on before, after, or during an event. Attribute categorizing can be thought of as comprehensive and allows for utilizing topics such as point of view, regional comparisons, and more. If done correctly, utilizing historical thinking skills in social studies students should focus on comparing significance of causes or effects, continuities and changes over time, contexts, and interpretations.

The second step is to make an executive decision, that is, the student needs to choose a conclusion based on the information they analyzed. When choosing between various categories previously compared, there are really only three choices that are possible, even if the categories are numerous or amounted to a dichotomy. The choices in evaluation are: "yes", "no", or "sometimes". Oftentimes this question manifests in a format that includes the phrasing: "to what extent." The possible conclusions to a prompt that includes an extent are: "to a large", "to a small", or "to no extent". The language associated with this execution is going to include a negation, a concession, or some other qualification to the evaluation the student concludes based on their assessment of quite often multifaceted comparisons. The most challenging evaluation to make is the qualified explanation, that of "sometimes" or "yes, but not always".

While not inclusive, some language that might be related to this threefold choice includes samples listed in the table below utilizing the four types of weighing. A, B, and C represent the topics that were weighed, and X represents a time period or event.

Categorization	Yes	No	Sometimes
Dichotomous	Yes, A is better than B	No, A is not better than B	A can be better than B given the right conditions
Thematic	A has more political conflicts than B or C.	A does not have more political conflicts than B or C.	A used to have more political conflicts than B or C, but those have been minimized
Time bound	Before X, A was stronger than B	Before X, A was in no better shape than B	Even though A saw greater change before X, B was not immune to X
Attribute	For A, occupation played a greater role than nationality	For A, occupation was not more impactful than nationality	For A, occupation was more impactful early in life, but nationality had a greater role later in life

In the chart above, observe how dichotomous evaluation weighs two topics (A and B). Thematic evaluation handles two or more topics (A, B, and C). Time bound evaluation considers topics in reference to specific events or eras (A and B in reference to X). Finally, attribute evaluation measures the topics against each other in reference to one topic (A).

To see this skill plat out in a more informal scenario, imagine a student must evaluate a simple dichotomous situation: whether to do homework or go to a movie with friends. To begin, the student does step one making a comparison chart that weighs the pros and cons of each activity to decide how to spend their limited free time as seen below.

Doing homework	Going to movie
Pros *+Practice skills* *+Prepared more for next test* *+Get feedback* *+Enhance skills* *+Guilt free* Cons *- Give up socializing on weekend* *- Left out of conversation about movie at school* *- Hard/Boring*	Pros *+Deepen friendships* *+Enjoy recreational activity* *+Tune out for a while and destress* Cons *- Miss practice on skill* *- Not as prepared for test next week* *- No feedback to get better next assignment* *- Guilt ruins movie, can't enjoy night out*

In this case, the student can easily recognize that there are five positive attributes to completing homework and only three drawbacks, whereas there are only three benefits to attending the movie, but four negative consequences of this choice. While this enumeration only accounts for the quantity of each consequence, of course a student would want to weigh the value of each consequence in terms of longevity of impact and other qualifying merit as well. So, in real life, students are evaluating on a regular basis. For personal decisions, the activity with the lowest amount of costs and the greatest benefits both quantitatively and qualitatively will often be chosen and executed. This student therefore has three possible conclusions he can draw after weighing the pros and cons:

Yes	No	Sometimes
I will go to the movie.	*I should not go to the movie and will do homework instead.*	*I might be able to go to the movie if I complete my work on time.*

Teaching the Students

Evaluation becomes more complex when other skills are employed in its execution often, a necessity in social studies education. Whereas students practice the skill subconsciously in their daily lives, to perform this skill with intent is a much harder process. Evaluation requires that they must simultaneously leverage, in tandem with evaluation, other historical thinking skills. To make things more difficult, true quality historical investigation should result in multiple correct answers to the same question. Indeed, qualified judgements about past events is the nature and essence of the discipline. "But what is the *right* answer?" will likely be a common question, particularly in the beginning of the year. It demonstrates that a nuanced question, with no obvious answer, has been posed that challenges the students. Bruce Lesh outlined high quality evaluative history lessons in his book "Why Won't You Just Tell Us the Answer?" Lesh (2011) suggests that asking evaluative questions about the text and subtext of primary sources helps students grapple with interpreting the historical record in refined ways.

Students should be constantly evaluating in the social studies classroom. Examples of opportunities for evaluation to manifest in the classroom include essential questions (Wiggins & McTighe, 2011), decision making activities (Silver et al., 2007), project topic selection, four corners activities, and ultimately, thesis writing. Any time students are given the opportunity to weigh historical evidence and then make a calculated decision about that evidence constitutes the practice of evaluation. Differentiating between *adopting* an opinion about a historical event and *forming* an educated opinion about historical evidence based on evaluation is a critical role for the invested educator.

Once students have been given relevant real-life examples of evaluation, the more nuanced historical examples can be shown. Consider the prompt: "Evaluate the greatest contributing factor to the Civil War." When evaluating the Civil War, students may feel at first as if they instinctively know the "right" answer based on a gut reaction or previous repeated exposure to the topic. Students might immediately suggest that slavery is the greatest cause of the Civil War. Yet, if students are trained in evaluation and paid attention in class when the subject was introduced, it also becomes defensible to argue that sectionalism, economic factors, or states' rights issues were the greatest cause of the Civil War. Being educated in the skill of evaluation should actually create tension, and maybe even a sense of panic, for students who cannot find an immediate path to the "right" answer because it becomes evident that there are often multiple right answers. As the student begins the process of weighing the evidence, they should build categories and fill in the evidence. In this case, thematic analysis is most appropriate as seen in the box below:

Social: slavery	**Regional:** sectionalism	**Economic:** industrialization	**Political:** states' rights
Abolitionism Second Great Awakening Expansion	*Competing value systems North v. South v. West*	*Alternatives to slave labor Export v. import dependent*	*Compromises Competing sovereignty between Federal and State*

Once the student has completed the task of weighing contributing factors according to isolated themes associated with the topic, the harder task of drawing a conclusion between competing choices forces the student to commit to a decision which completes the skill of evaluation. To reach this step, students need to first audit each thematic category and decide whether it is a major cause (Yes), it is not as major of a cause (No), or it might be a major cause (Sometimes). Once the field of possible thematic conclusions has been narrowed to two "Yes" answers, the students then need to choose between those two themes and decide "Yes" to one, and "No" to the other. They also have the option to reconcile the best two responses by qualifying the response as "Sometimes". By practicing metacognition, a student can decide which statement is more true based on the categories compared and select a conclusion that is easiest to defend based on the weighing of evidence. See the table below related to the previous prompt:

Yes	Yes	Sometimes
Slavery was the greatest contributing factor to the Civil War. *(No to political issues)*	*Political issues were the single greatest contributing factor to the Civil War.* *(No to slavery issues)*	*Slavery was a contributing social factor to the Civil War, but political issues surrounding states' rights was the greatest contributing factor to start the war.*

Both the weighing, through systematic categorization, and choosing, based on the "yes, no, sometimes" conclusions, are helpful in breaking down the steps associated with evaluation. An anchor chart for the wall of the classroom can help students remember the basic steps associated with this complex skill as shown below:

Evaluation (E)

Student can discern that evaluation is being assessed, can appropriately weigh and choose between potential arguments, events and ideas that relate to the assigned task.

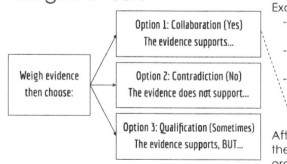

Weigh evidence then choose:

Option 1: Collaboration (Yes)
The evidence supports...

Option 2: Contradiction (No)
The evidence does not support...

Option 3: Qualification (Sometimes)
The evidence supports, BUT...

Example:
- A graph shows that orange trees grow better in warm climates like Florida.
- Orange trees planted in Michigan have died because of the winters.
- There is not enough natural rainfall in desert climates to provide enough water to keep an orange tree healthy.

After weighing these facts, the evidence supports the argument that it is likely a good idea to plant orange trees in Florida.

When it comes to constructing an essay response, the evaluation skill is only weighing information and deciding what the argument is going to be. However, the argumentation skill is the ability to write a response defending that choice. That defense requires a line of reasoning within a purposefully constructed thesis as well as elaboration on supporting evidence, both of which are discussed in Chapter 11: Argumentation.

Troubleshooting

Student Misconception 1: Choice paralysis

Oftentimes as students are developing executive decision-making skills, they will find themselves unable to commit to a choice preferring to endlessly weigh their options. Perhaps this is because in daily life they are making easy dichotomous decisions. There is a good or bad choice, essentially a better or worse solution that students are asked to find. The diametric nature of so many personal evaluations can lead students to draw more shallow conclusions about historical evaluations, and they will thus be uncomfortable with more dynamic decisions due to inexperience. Rigorous social studies instruction requires students to consider a variety of criteria in evaluation. When instructing students to think more broadly or more deeply about the topic, it can be helpful for them to focus on placing a value on itemized characteristics with unequal merit. Essentially, help the students decide which information about the topic holds the most relevance and use that to help make their choice.

However, in looking at the level of significance of items being weighed students can still feel frozen by indecision and hesitate to commit to a stance as they fear they are wrong and a choice cannot be undone. Students then tend to equivocate, trying to claim multiple choices are right answers rather than evaluate and commit to a justified response. It may be that students struggle because they did not weigh effectively, or they may have ineffectively employed the other historical thinking skills. Difficulty weighing contextualized information, utilizing cause and effect, or comparing evidence on the topic will hinder their ability to analyze before they make a choice. Students will be able to come to a conclusion once they effectively weigh and rank the significance of the information in their analysis. To encourage this have them revisit the analysis step to help students complete the choice phase of evaluation. Thus, more valuable, insightful and higher quality evaluations will be made by the students. It is also important to remember that nuanced evaluation may very well be a new skill for students, and just like other new skills, it will require repeated exposure and practice to improve.

Student Misconception 2: Predisposition to singularity of a "right" answer

After years of being told there is a singular right answer to every question, students may feel frustrated with or even afraid of the idea that there are multiple right answers to historical questions. This frustration needs to be normalized for students as a characteristic of evaluation. By *acknowledging* the difficulty of the task assigned and *validating* the students' frustration, teachers can move the student from a state of tension to a solution-focused mode of thinking. Students need to be reassured that they are capable of performing the task based on all of their practice and reminded they are qualified to offer a claim based on their participation in the class. By borrowing the teacher's confidence in them as historians and telling them that there is no single correct answer, the student can then develop their own confidence in their abilities.

The social-emotional needs of the students play a critical role in their ability to overcome choice paralysis and their fear of answering the question "wrong". Fostering a growth mindset will encourage the students to develop the confidence to try and answer a question, even if it is not the best answer or the one the teacher would have picked. In general, a whole class approach should be established to normalize evaluative thinking. Yet, many of these more intimate conversations about a student's social and emotional concerns in addressing the difficulties of evaluation will likely occur in small groups or one-on-one tutoring scenarios given the sensitivity and vulnerability required to overcome these challenges.

When it comes to the mechanics of implementing solutions to the above mentioned concerns there are a variety of logistical techniques to be employed in the classroom. One technique that can be used is to help the student focus on vocabulary cues inherent in the prompt. For example, highlight how "better" (compared to one item) and "best" (compared to multiple items) do not have the same meaning. Similarly, how "most" implies a majority, but not the entirety, can offer clues to the student as to how to approach their conclusion. By evaluating the semantics of the task, students can expand beyond their traditional dichotomous approach and broaden their thinking to encompass more creative solutions and generate higher quality evaluations. In addition, often highlighting the variety of answers, particularly the outlier responses, that classmates offered to the same question will also encourage healthy risk-taking and creative thinking in submissions.

Importance of Evaluation

Inherent in the skill of evaluation, is also the practicing of the skill comparison, and often causation, or even continuity and change over time. The prerequisite of having competency in earlier skills to effectively evaluate does indeed make evaluation a more advanced skill than it might at first appear. Direct instruction in how the skill works, coupled with opportunities to practice drawing informed conclusions based on well executed evaluation will allow students to become better overall decision makers. Because this skill is required in everyday tasks, becoming more proficient in the nuances associated with executing the skill is a transfer goal of all social studies classrooms. Understanding that there are multiple right answers to many of life's questions will be liberating for students if communicated effectively and practiced in the safe environment of the social studies lab.

Reconciling the idea that people will come to different conclusions with the same information will help them better empathize and discuss more difficult topics in their everyday lives. With formal training in this skill, adults can go on to make better evaluations of college degree programs, political office candidates, mortgage rates, and potential career paths. This will ensure adults will enjoy a much more fulfilling personal and professional life, with fewer individual, societal, financial, and occupational costs.

Social Studies Examples

World Geography prompt:
"Which factor of climate has the greatest impact in creating the Atacama Desert?"

Factor 1	Factor 2	Factor 3	Factor 4	Factor 5
Latitude Just above Tropic of Capricorn in "Hot" Zone Lots of direct sunlight	**Ocean Currents** Humboldt Current brings cold water, cools off the air on coast	**Wind Currents** Prevailing winds move east to west, making it difficult for storms to come off the coast	**Elevation** High elevation in the Andes Mountains, makes it cold	**Landforms** Andes Mountains and eastern trade winds create a Rain Shadow Effect, keeping it dry
Student Response: *The Andes Mountain landform has the greatest impact in creating the Atacama Desert.*				

World History prompt:
"Which factor influenced the Allied victory in World War II the most?"

Topic 1	Topic 2	Topic 3
demographics Decline in births due to war separations of couples Increase in deaths due to war Movement to cities for industrial production	**technology** Advances in airplane bombers Advances in machine guns Zyklon B gas use in holocaust camps Atomic bomb development and use	**economics** Worldwide Great Depression US Lend-Lease Act German hyperinflation National War Production Boards
Student Response: *The most significant factor to influence the Allied victory in World War II was the advancements in technology.*		

United States History prompt:

"When did the intellectual aspect of the American Revolution begin?"

Era 1	Era 2	Era 3
Early Colonial Period Virginia House of Burgesses 1619 Mayflower Compact 1620 Establishment of self-rule in colonies	**Early/Mid-18th Century** Disregard for Proclamation of 1763 First congress of colonies at Albany	**Revolutionary Era** Stamp Act Crisis escalated and organized protests First colony-wide unified rejection of British rule in Declaration of Independence
Student Response: *The intellectual aspect of the American Revolution began when the colonies were first established.*		

Government prompt:

"Which linkage institution is most influential in elections?"

Group 1	Group 2	Group 3
political parties Party platform development National conventions Watchdog function Organizing campaign efforts	**media** Investigative journalism Poll results reporting Campaign advertising	**interest groups** Lobbying Litigation Grassroots movements Electioneering
Student Response: *The most influential linkage institution when it comes to elections is interest groups.*		

Economics prompt:

"Are demand determinants the most influential factors on marketplace dynamics?"

Yes	No	Sometimes
Demand Preferences and tastes Expectations Number of buyers Taxes Consumer income Alternative products	**Supply** Taxes Suppliers in the market Technology Profits in other markets Resource costs Expectations	**both** Expectations Taxes Number of participants
Student Response: *The most influential determinants of marketplace dynamics are shared by both supply and demand.*		

Psychology prompt:

"Was Bandura's Bobo Doll experiment ethical?"

Yes	No	Maybe
Any learned negative behavior would eventually go extinct so no long-term damage to children	It is wrong to try to teach children to be aggressive in all cases	How much the children picked up aggressive behaviors was not known as experiment began

Student Response: *Bandura's Bobo Doll experiment was not ethical.*

Evaluation (E) Reflection

Here are some metacognitive questions to get started with reflection:

1. How has your understanding of evaluation changed after reading this chapter?

2. How can you support students social and emotional vulnerability as they practice these new skills?

3. Where do you anticipate your students having the most misunderstandings and what scaffolding will they need when introduced to the skill?

4. What steps do you need to take to increase your confidence in generating and grading evaluation prompts?

5. How will you implement the evaluation skill in a lesson in your classroom?

Chapter 10:
Synthesis (S)

Skill Overview
Synthesis is arguably the most difficult skill as it requires students to create an original connection between disparate ideas. There are three types of synthesis, in increasing difficulty based on how much the student is asked to do. Advanced comparison is the easiest synthesis as it asks students to find a connection between topics that is not as obvious as basic comparison, but is still structured, such as grouping documents for a DBQ. The next type of synthesis is comparative synthesis where two disparate topics are given, and the student must create a connection between them. The most difficult is innovative synthesis where the teacher gives a topic and the student must not only generate another topic to connect to, but also build the connection itself.

How To
Type 1: Advanced Comparison
    Finding a connection between structured topic given
Type 2: Comparative Synthesis
    Two disparate topics given, need to create connections between them
Type 3: Innovative Synthesis
    One topic given, need to generate a disparate topic and create connections between them

Graphic Organizer

Topic	Disparate Topic if provided: synthesized comparison if created: innovative synthesis	Connection

Sentence Stems
Difficult to use sentence stems for, so instead give the students themes, like SPICE, to pick from as topics for connections.

Example
Making a cake is a lot like writing an essay. Not only do you have to have the right ingredients, whether it is eggs, flour and sugar, or context, details and evidence, but you also need to add them in the right order, just as wet ingredients need mix before dry ingredients are added, the body paragraph should not come before the intro paragraph. Finally, the product is dependent on the quality of ingredients used in both; with fresh vanilla instead of imitation vanilla, a cake tastes better, just as with accurate and specific details an essay is better argued and defended. Both are more pleasing to each respective audience when done well.

Introduction to Synthesis

When researchers modified the original Bloom's Taxonomy in 2001, they made two important changes regarding synthesis. First, they broadened Bloom's word choice of "Synthesis" to "Creating". Second, they decided that "Creating" should be higher on the taxonomy than "Evaluating" because it is more difficult to do. This book's system of historical thinking skills uses the word "Synthesis" rather than "Creating," but keeps it at the top of the taxonomy acknowledging its difficulty.

One reason for this choice is the general ambiguity about what creation looks like in the classroom. Too often, simple activities such as creating a poster or diorama are labelled "creating", when all the students were asked to do was recall, understand, or apply information to complete the task. Therefore, these assignments are *not* true creation, as indicated on Bloom's Taxonomy, and thus lead to student and teacher confusion about performance levels of critical thinking. The synthesis skill does involve creation, but as a critical thinking skill this refers to *creating* patterns and meaning out of seemingly disparate parts. Utilizing the word "synthesis" helps to maintain rigor and clarity in critical thinking expectations of students.

It should be noted that creating is so inherent to more advanced synthesis that one could argue that the skill is actually the metacognition of creating. However, the various degrees of difficulty within synthesis can cause confusion. Indeed, over time synthesis as a skill has been misunderstood, reorganized, or even diluted because of its complexity. Yet synthesis is a necessary and relevant skill that, like analysis and evaluation, is often utilized in everyday life.

With synthesis, despite its complexity, this skill is the one most likely to just "happen to" students in a passive way without their awareness. It may be experienced as a feeling of deja vu, or a sudden "lightbulb moment" connection between topics. Often this presents as a moment in class where a student boisterously exclaims about a connection that just occurred to them between a movie or song they remember and the topic being discussed. In historical application, synthesis is much less likely to occur naturally and often requires repeated modeling and practice in order to employ this skill on command and at will. Educators, having been exposed to so much more content over the course of their lives are much more likely to see connections in the processes of historical repetition. However, students will struggle as their context is limited and their retention of previous exposure to historical knowledge may be weaker due to a lack of significance or salience when acquiring prior knowledge. The task then is to teach the students how to do such difficult abstract thinking on command.

How the Skill Works

Focusing too much practice on the more easily accessible degrees of synthesis, or what will be called here, advanced comparison, can limit students' abilities to fully develop one of the paramount skills needed of adults in the 21st century: innovation. For this reason, differentiating the various degrees of synthesis is of the utmost importance when utilizing this skill so that innovative synthesis and synthesized comparison can be taught purposefully. There are three levels to the depth of synthesis: advanced comparison, synthesized comparison, and innovative synthesis. These levels of difficulty are graduated and become more complex based on how independent the students are in their contribution to the thinking and creating.

Synthesis can seem remarkably close to the comparison skill in that the created connections and patterns are essentially complex similarities drawn between topics. Basic comparison, which was covered in Chapter 5, is describing the similarities and differences between two topics and drawing a conclusion. Topics for comparison are often very thematically similar, for example an exercise in comparison may call for the students to compare the New England and Southern American colonies. Similarities and differences on this topic would be easy to isolate, such as the purpose for creating the colonies, who started the colonies, and where the colonies focused their economy.

The advanced comparison level of synthesis asks the students to draw connections that are not as obvious. For example, given a DBQ prompt comparing the colonies, the connections and grouping of themes students create between the given documents would be a more advanced comparison because it requires students to understand the document, utilize context, create theme titles that can be applied to multiple documents, and finally answer a prompt. The act of creating theme titles and connecting the documents to answer a prompt requires much more difficult cognition than a simple comparison.

The degree to which advanced comparison is truly synthesis can be debated, but for the purposes of this system of historical thinking skills it is considered the most simplified version of synthesis. Advanced comparison is necessary to the classroom; however, for the purposes of synthesis it best acts as a scaffolding measure to teach abstract connections.

The next level of difficulty in the synthesis skill is synthesized comparison. Synthesized comparison occurs when students describe similarities between disparate topics that are provided by the teacher. For example, asking the students to synthesize between the American Southern Colonies and the Belgian Colonies of the Congo would be significantly more complex because of the extent of disparity between the topics. Instinctually, students will connect that both titles of the topics have the word "colonies" in them and they may try to propose that the connection is that they are both colonies, providing the definition of colonies to refine their comparison. However, these are actually fairly disparate topics because they are on different continents, run by different countries, with different resources, and exist in different time periods. An example of a quality connection is that both colonial systems enslaved Africans and cruelly punished them, perpetuating a racist class system. Asking students to find similarities between disparate topics will be a significant challenge at first, but through repetition and practice it will extend their ability to identify and label connections to help move them closer to innovative synthesis.

The most difficult level of synthesis is innovative synthesis because it requires the most complex thinking from the student. The degree of difficulty for students is determined by how much the student is expected to create and do themselves. Innovative synthesis requires students to generate a disparate topic to compare *and* articulate connections. To do this, the student is required to create a new and unique theory of connection, but one which exhibits similar functions and characteristics in a completely novel way.

Offering students a topic and asking them where they have seen similar circumstances before should over time elicit innovative synthesis. Using the example of the American colonies, a student would be performing innovative synthesis if, without any prompting from the teacher, they suggest that the jealous and competitive nature of the American colonies amongst each other is similar to the jealous and competitive nature between Greek city-states. This is a much more disparate comparison and demands that the student not only generate a topic to compare but to create an original connection between two distinctly different topics from two different subjects across both time and space and thus, exhibits innovative synthesis. In fact, connections can even be made to non-historical topics and across other academic disciplines, or even from historical issues to current events. A table is provided below that organizes the above referenced examples to help students delineate the various depths of synthesis:

	Comparison	Synthesized Comparison	Innovative Synthesis
Extent of Student Involvement	Teacher provides topics with fairly easy connections; student describes similarities and differences	Teacher provides disparate topics; student generates connection between them	Teacher provides a topic; student generates second topic and makes original connection
Example: Topic(s) Provided by Teacher	New England and Southern American Colonies	American Southern Colonies and Belgian Congo	Jealousy and competition between American Colonies created tension
Example: Student Response/ Connection	*The colonies differed in how they made money in each region, but were all British culturally so each American colony was impacted by the Enlightenment*	*Both enslaved Africans and cruelly punished them, perpetuating a racist class system*	*City-state jealousy and competition in Ancient Greece created tension among city-states too, so that complex relationship is similar to the one between the American Colonies*

By providing the students with a table like the one on the previous page, they can more easily see the level at which they are performing synthesis. This kind of visual resource also can provide them with examples of stretch goals for growing in their ability to perform this skill. Yet, direct instruction should not be limited to analysis of levels of synthesis; students must have the skill modeled and have opportunities for practice.

Teaching the Students

When introducing any skill, the best segway into creating relevance for the student is to highlight where they have already experienced or practiced the skill. In fact, students are exposed to the practice of synthesis in a variety of ways quite naturally through pervasive social media. For example, students regularly enjoy the humor associated with social media memes. So much so, they are likely to pass particularly entertaining ones on to friends. Memes are a clear example of synthesis and can help facilitate both abstract synthesis and innovative synthesis. In order for a student to appreciate and find humor in a meme, they have to already understand the context from prior knowledge regarding the meme template. Then they must practice abstract synthesis as they connect the template context to the text content referenced, interpreting disparate ideas to appreciate the humor. To reach the higher level of synthesis, students can generate their own meme by taking an image template and writing a remark in the text associated, which creates a completely new connection between content and pop culture. A task like this assigned to students can introduce them to the accessibility of even the most complex level of innovative synthesis in a more accessible, yet relevant manner. Memes are a great resource to use in the classroom for highlighting, in a concrete way, how the synthesis skill manifests.

Internalizing the Skills

Unlike traditional instruction where the content is always changing, allowing for excitement and variety in new units, with a skills-based approach I sometimes felt like I was eating, breathing, and sleeping with the skills. There was no escape. I saw skills in movies, I read skills in news articles, I saw skills in interactions in the grocery store. What I did not realize is the benefit this would have for my students. My first year, I started by looking at upcoming content and selecting a skill to highlight over the course of that week. Sometimes the content lent itself more readily to a couple of skills and it was easy to decide where I would focus my attention during instruction. When I effectively internalized the skills, it became so much easier to weave them into every conversation and focus on them relentlessly, which eventually became quite natural, but only after a couple of years into using this system. I think it's important to accept that with skills-based teaching you are never "done" teaching any one skill. I was always helping refine student's understanding of how the skills work together in limitless ways, even with students who had a teacher using this system in previous years. Only then did I start to see not just the professional, but also the personal benefits of living a skills life, both in and out of my classroom."

– Tillotson

Helping students build meaningful connections between history and modern events utilizing synthesis will provide relevancy to content and practice transferring historical thinking skills to life outside of a classroom. Abstract connections between historical events and similar circumstances in the United States and around the world during the 21st century, may appear evident once explained by the teacher. Yet, making these connections independently is a significant leap for the untrained student and will require tremendous practice and repetition for students to be able to perform independent synthesis with current events. Structured practice of this skill is critical to gaining student interest in content, utilizing skills in a relevant context, and practicing transfer goals.

Another very convenient technique for encouraging innovative synthesis is to leverage English language skills which students have already been introduced to in their English classes. Creating analogies, allusions, idioms, metaphors, and allegories all represent innovative synthesis that allow students to understand one topic in terms of another. In English course work, students have been asked to recognize these techniques authors utilize in literature; asking students to generate them in social studies is a way to scaffold innovative synthesis using their prior knowledge from another discipline.

If students are struggling to describe connections between disparate topics, they can utilize social studies themes as a common language. The students can use any teacher chosen acronym for themes, such as SPICE (Social, Political, Interactions with the Environment, Cultural, Economic), as a system to audit patterns they observe. An anchor chart like the one below can highlight the process of utilizing themes to support synthesis at various levels:

Synthesis (S)

Student can discern that synthesis is being assessed, and can make connections between a given issue and related developments in a different context.

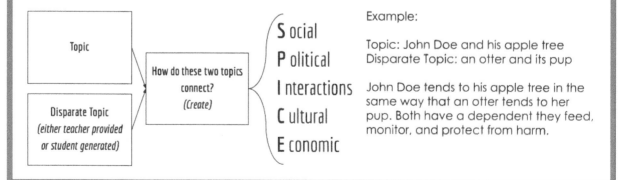

Topic		**S** ocial	Example:
How do these two topics connect? (*Create*)		**P** olitical	Topic: John Doe and his apple tree
Disparate Topic (*either teacher provided or student generated*)		**I** nteractions	Disparate Topic: an otter and its pup
		C ultural	John Doe tends to his apple tree in the same way that an otter tends to her pup. Both have a dependent they feed, monitor, and protect from harm.
		E conomic	

Oftentimes, students will get the best practice in synthesis when completing performance assessments. For example, asking students to create a visual art piece about a subject can require them to synthesize. In a scenario where a student paints an abstract piece about the Civil War, there are several steps they will need to take to complete the task. They will need to first understand and analyze the content by breaking it down into meaningful pieces. Then they need to take those meaningful pieces of historical content and translate them into symbolism and a cohesive theme. However, the students need to be able to articulate the symbolism being employed by writing a paragraph explaining their synthesized connections in order to exhibit their awareness of the metacognition they practiced to arrive at the final product. The students will find creating art to be the easy part, but explaining how they innovated by creating meaning from historical content proves to be more difficult, and is thus the more important endeavor.

Another technique to use in teaching synthesis is to assign investigations that are conducted independently which allow students freedom of both process and product. Independent investigations of compelling content, initiated based on student interests, allow for more depth of research than is offered in class. To do an independent investigation, students are given a list of individual historical figures, key events, significant vocabulary, or even a general time period as a springboard for beginning a more extensive self-directed research project. Helping students craft a question to research and facilitating Socratic conversations about what their research has allowed them to conclude can teach students how to find pride in performing argumentation about the research conducted independently. These performance assessments can manifest as mock newspaper editions, hypothetical soliloquies of historical figures, original works of art, several page long essays, or any host of other products based on student interest and inherent abilities. Giving the student agency over the selection of the product to exhibit their argumentation affords students the opportunity to practice innovative synthesis with the teacher as a facilitator. This encourages independent innovative synthesis and allows practice of transfer goals using historical thinking skills.

Troubleshooting

Student Misconception 1: Underdeveloped prerequisite skills

It is critical to remember that synthesis is at the very top of Bloom's Taxonomy for a reason: it is the highest level of critical thinking and thus requires the greatest effort due to its complexity. Indeed, in order to complete synthesis properly students must employ virtually all the other levels in the taxonomy. Students must recall, understand, and apply the content, analyze the content for meaning by breaking it down into parts to compare, analyze the context of each topic, and finally evaluate the relevancy of each part to construct a connection. Unfortunately, this means that if students are not proficient in any of the other skills, they will find it difficult to synthesize.

In order to help students overcome these deficiencies, the teacher should isolate which skills specifically the student is struggling with and address them appropriately using the suggestions offered in previous chapters. Once students have had some successful practice with analysis and evaluation, provide scaffolding for synthesis utilizing advanced comparison or thematic audits regarding two topics with which the student is most familiar. One suggestion for how to isolate which skill or process the student is struggling with is to walk the student through a meme or another synthesized comparison example in a one-on-one format after the student professes, "I don't get it." With a meme, for example, if the student does not understand how to interpret the template picture, they are struggling with contextualization; whereas if they do not understand the added text, it may be a Lower Bloom's content issue. If the student understands both the template and the text but cannot connect them, it is a synthesis issue.

The student may resist such in depth analysis of something that is supposed to be light and humorous; however, it is critical when teaching such complex skills that the teacher not only practices, but models the metacognition they want the students to learn. A particularly exciting breakthrough from one-on-one experiences as referenced above, with student permission, can then be translated to a whole group clarification and even remediation of skills.

Student Misconception 2: Teacher vs. student centered synthesis

With synthesis it is critical to be cognizant of exactly what work the teacher and the students are doing in the process of the skill. Common concerns regarding synthesis usually relate to ownership of the mental energy expended in completing the skill or task. When assigning topics, it is the teacher's role to be aware of exactly how disparate the topics actually are as that is proportional to how difficult the analysis will be for the students. If students struggle with topics that are more loosely related, scaffolding of advanced comparison will allow the teacher to build support for more synthesized comparison. From there, the student can be advanced to more disparate topics. The synthesis should become more and more student generated over time.

In addition, teachers must also reflect on and mitigate what shortcuts the students may take to avoid the difficult brain work involved in synthesizing. Students may try to just extend analysis that the teacher has already showcased instead of creating an original connection or may claim credit for connections already alluded to by their peers or in lessons. If the student, whether they realize it or not, circumvents the creation aspect of synthesizing, it is important to help the student understand the originality component necessary to synthesis. By clarifying the level of synthesis being attempted and being achieved, students will more likely attempt more complex levels of synthesis. Over time, with exhibited metacognition on the teacher's part, students will adopt this habit of mind and will practice their own metacognition. This will allow the student to more accurately attribute ownership of thinking to its source of origin allowing them to think more about a topic to originate their own innovative synthesis.

Importance of Synthesis

Innovative synthesis is truly the transfer goal of this skill as it can be used in college research, career paths, and the rest of adult life. Even in scientific research and with many technological advancements in industry, the practice of creating connections makes people more innovative and therefore, more employable. For example, synthetic oils and synthetic fabrics are completely new and original iterations of a previously known product, yet fulfill a similar function, thus are examples of innovative synthesis. In all cases, an individual generates a completely new and original iteration of information learned but which exhibits the same functions or characteristics in a completely novel way. This is the skill that throughout history has allowed new polymers to be invented, new methods of communication to be developed, and new coping mechanisms to be employed for a better world today, tomorrow, and well into the future.

Social Studies Examples

World Geography topic: Mountain Ranges

Topic	Disparate Topic if provided: synthesized comparison if created: innovative synthesis	Connection
Himalayan Mountains	Mediterranean Sea	**Student Response:** *Regardless of their physical makeup, large landforms can encourage cultural isolation which can be seen in both Russian vs. South Asian culture and Southern European vs. North African culture*

World History topic: World War II

Topic	Disparate Topic if provided: synthesized comparison if created: innovative synthesis	Connection
Nazi party's rise to power in 1933	President Vladmir Putin of Russia in the 21st century	**Student Response:** *Both practiced authoritarian government actions against activism and resistance with Ukrainians in place of Jews as well as extremism generating political divisiveness worldwide.*

United States History topic: The American Revolution

Topic	Disparate Topic if provided: synthesized comparison if created: innovative synthesis	Connection
Military strategy in the American Revolution	Military strategy during the Vietnam War	**Student Response:** *Both are examples of a more advanced country's military facing difficulty combatting local farmers and militiamen who knew the terrain better and employed guerrilla warfare.*

Government topic: Constitution

Topic	Disparate Topic if provided: synthesized comparison if created: innovative synthesis	Connection
The Supreme Court usually aligns with the previous administration	Financial outcomes are inherited from an earlier administration	**Student Response:** *Both influence policy decisions based on ideology or outcomes generated by a different administration so to some extent, policymaking is limited under any current executive administration.*

Economics prompt: Supply and Demand

Topic	Disparate Topic if provided: synthesized comparison if created: innovative synthesis	Connection
Law of Supply: as prices rise quantity demanded falls	To engage a manual transmission, the clutch is released as the gas pedal is compressed	**Student Response:** *As one decreases, the other must inversely increase in an opposing, "see-saw" like fashion.*

Psychology prompt: Classical Conditioning

Topic	Disparate Topic if provided: synthesized comparison if created: innovative synthesis	Connection
Little Albert Experiment: classically conditioned fear in a child	Due to a recent car crash where a student was hit by a drunk driver in the rain, the student now feels anxious whenever driving in the rain	**Student Response:** *In both cases, the participant has a fear reaction to the stimulus without causal factors (mice are not harmful and rain is not dangerous) due to classical conditioning.*

Synthesis (S) Reflection

Here are some metacognitive questions to get started with reflection:

1. How has your understanding of synthesis (and creating) changed after reading this chapter?

2. What do you think your students' reaction will be to these new revelations about synthesis?

3. Where do you anticipate your students having the most misunderstandings and what scaffolding will they need when introduced to the skill?

4. What steps do you need to take to increase your confidence in generating and grading synthesized comparison prompts and recognizing innovative synthesis?

5. How will you implement the synthesis skill in a lesson in your classroom?

Chapter 11:

Argumentation

Introduction to Argumentation

Argumentation can be used with all skills, across skills, and interdependently within the skills. Argumentation is unique in that it is not a targeted skill to assess in isolation. It simply cannot be conducted without employing the other skills. In this way, argumentation formats the application of every skill. In the critical thinking skill-focused classroom, argumentation becomes a basic modality of skill use. Thus, specifically grading the other seven skills is more efficient and productive. Formative feedback can be given on argumentation while simultaneously maintaining the priority of assessing the student's proficiency in the historical thinking skills. For example, given a prompt asking for the students to assess the causes of a war, the grade and feedback will be given on the quality of the causal relationship, while additional narrative feedback on use of evidence and formatting can be given to supplement argumentation as a means of communicating skill proficiency.

At its core, argumentation is the active justification of a claim. Usually, as it manifests in the social studies classroom, it includes a thesis comprised of a claim and a line of reasoning, as well as some elaboration on the rationale supporting the line of reasoning. An anchor chart can help remind students of the components required in making an argument, as seen on the next page:

Argumentation

The student can articulate a defensible claim in the form of a clear and compelling thesis that evaluates the importance of multiple factors and can support the argument through close analysis and use of relevant and diverse evidence, framing the argument and evidence around a thinking skill.

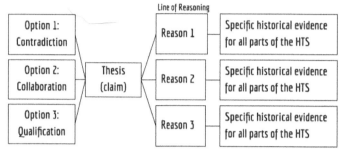

Example: *Although X, Y. This is evidenced by A, B, and C.*

While orange trees can grow in other states, it is likely a good idea to plant orange trees in Florida. This is evidenced by Florida's sufficient natural rainfall to support the growth of orange trees, its consistent year round sunlight to encourage tree growth, and its nutrient rich soil to facilitate fruit production.

For the purposes of this system of thinking, a conclusion is the processed results of one targeted skill. A claim is different and more complex in that it merges multiple conclusions in order to answer a prompt. Once students can create an argument, explaining their reasoning in a paragraph is the most basic formatting. An essay would be a more advanced system of formatting. See the chart below:

Argumentation Building Blocks
Conclusion = processed results of analysis using a targeted skill
Claim = a merging of multiple conclusions
Line of reasoning = organized evidence to support claim
Thesis = claim + line of reasoning
Paragraph = argumentation in its most basic format
Essay = argumentation in a more advanced format

Integration of Multiple Historical Thinking Skills

Ultimately, higher academia and career work will not pose critical thinking skills in isolation. Once students have had sufficient practice with the thinking skills separately, they should be asked to employ more than one skill at a time. Students should find this more difficult as answering a prompt with more than one skill required will ask them to reconcile multiple conclusions drawn from various skills in order to formulate a cohesive claim. For example, advanced prompts may ask for the causes of changes over time, to compare interpretations, or to evaluate the effects of a given time period, issue, or event. Initially, students will struggle with argumentation as it will generally require the dexterous employment of more than one skill simultaneously. However, real world application in the university or advanced career level is rarely as simple as utilizing one skill, idea, or thought process in a singular fashion. Therefore, it is critical to challenge students by requiring them to integrate more than one skill at a time.

In order to help the students break down and process more difficult prompts like those offered in advanced classes, consistent and varied scaffolding is required. It should be noted that the teacher ought to focus on employing multiple skills only after previously introduced skills are practiced in a targeted manner. Once the students are proficient in the individual skills, additional instruction can be employed in integrating more than one skill at a time. For example, in a prompt asking for the causes of changes over time, the teacher can break down separately for the class the causal relationships and the changes over time in the era of the prompt. Then the teacher can model how the skills work together, in this case how the changes become the effects in the causation formula. This will build student confidence utilizing scaffolding outlined in previous chapters.

> ### Spiral Teaching
>
> "I learned about spiral teaching in the early days of my training as an educator. I understood the idea behind teaching in a spiral pattern even then, but I don't think I actually appreciated the significance it could have in the success of students until I adopted a skills-based ideology. Spiral teaching is in essence ensuring that with each revolution, whether it is a chapter, a unit, or an era, standards are strategically repeated. The way I was originally taught, the intersecting points of repetition would represent advanced synthesis, comparing different time periods for 'history repeating itself'. However, this is a content focused system of spiral teaching. I knew the repetitive nature of instruction using this method should not be abandoned, so I superimposed an additional spiral of skills. Each lesson, chapter, and unit become an opportunity to leverage fresh content for new practice on the same skills. This repetition is foundational to a skills-based classroom and provides not only continuity of development of the skills, but another categorical way to study social studies as the skills themselves intersect too. Educators practicing self-reflection can enhance their metacognition when envisioning how to use spiral teaching, not just out of necessity, but intentionally."
>
> – Tillotson

One of the best student-centered strategies for scaffolding complex prompt processing is to have the students break down each phrase in the prompt to see which skills need to be used, what the context for the prompt is, and what topics to focus on. Initially, this will need to be modeled a few times, but with practice, this technique will become a routine internal dialogue for students to utilize and even record as they work through each prompt. In these most complex iterations of multiple skill use, students' level of metacognition becomes critical to the process. See the example below for a skill breakdown of a prompt:

Prompt: "Evaluate to what extent the Second Great Awakening that occurred in the United States in the 19th century led to changes in American society."

Prompt Elements	Student Metacognition Assessing Prompt
Evaluate	*Weigh and choose*
to what extent	*How much? Options: a lot, a little, not at all*
the Second Great Awakening that occurred	*19th century religious revival that led to many reform movements and early Progressivism*
in the United States in the 19th century	*All information used must relate to the US in the 1800s only*
led to	*Analyze using cause -> how -> effects.*
changes	*The Second Great Awakening is the cause so focus should be on the effects of the movement. Need to figure out if those effects were big = change or small = continuity*
in American	*Limit response to America only, no international affairs*
society.	*People's interactions with each other*

Another immensely helpful scaffolding strategy, once the context, topics, and skills in the prompt have been isolated and identified, is to encourage the students to then reword the prompt in more student friendly language. So, the prompt given above, in more discernible student-friendly language, becomes easier to decode as seen on the next page:

> **Student Reframing:** *Weigh and choose how much this religious revival created effects in the US in the 1800s in how people interacted with each other in America.*

A further refined example from a more experienced student might be:

> **Student Reframing:** *How much did the 2nd Great Awakening create change or continuity in the way people acted?*

The prompt provided above may seem short or straightforward at first glance, but, as seen in the breakdown, it is actually quite complex because the students are asked to employ a majority of the higher order thinking skills to answer it. First, they must use contextualization in order to know what eras and topics they are analyzing. Then they need to analyze the *effects* of the topic using causation, while in tandem considering change and continuity over time as they assess the *changes* of the time period. Because the prompt asks them to "evaluate", they must also weigh the significance of the relationship between effects and changes. Finally, to create their claim, they need to choose "to what extent", or how much, of an impact the *effects* of the movement had on society. Only once the student analyzes and evaluates the context, topic, and skills required of a prompt and has drawn multiple conclusions, can they attempt to coherently express their argument in formal writing.

Building a Thesis Using the Skills

While there are a variety of conclusions students must draw as they diagnose a prompt for individual skills, their ultimate argument and thesis will begin with their claim followed by a line of reasoning. It is imperative that students keep their historical thinking skills in mind as they formulate theses to answer complex prompts so that they can more easily process the expectations. Unless the students establish a line of reasoning using the historical thinking skills first, the claim will be less effective or indefensible. When addressing a prompt students first need to use the thinking skills to organize evidence which will allow them to categorize prior knowledge within the context of the prompt. This organization allows students to create groupings and draw conclusions about those characteristics of evidence that become the line of reasoning to support their claim, both of which are combined to make up a thesis.

In the simplest demonstration of a line of reasoning, students can group evidence to address a prompt by employing language associated with the skills. Alternatively, when there are too many skills required to focus on the language of only one skill, students can group evidence in topical categories. The language of each skill combined with category topics can guide the grouping exercise and help the students more directly answer the prompt as seen in the table on the next page.

Focus Skill	Common Skill Language
Causation	due to, as a result, led to, caused, created, affected, impacted
Comparison	similar, different, larger, longer, least, most
CCOT	continuity, change, before, during, after, early, middle, late, increased, decreased
Other Options	Examples include: themes (social, economic, political, cultural, intellectual, geographic) interpretation (authorship, audience, purpose, point of view) regional (domestic, international, stage of development, rural, urban)

Once students have grouped evidence and drawn a conclusion they can develop a thesis which includes both a claim (a merging of their conclusions) and a line of reasoning (groupings of evidence). Based on an evaluation of grouped evidence in the era and topic, the students create a claim by corroborating, contradicting, or qualifying their response to the prompt. Most students will usually corroborate with a prompt by presenting evidence that supports it. Sometimes, a student will contradict a prompt by using evidence that disproves a statement. The most advanced method is to qualify a prompt, by presenting both supporting and contradicting evidence which leans toward one of those perspectives. In other words, a "Yes, but…" response. Although students may find difficulty in qualifying a prompt at first, it is good practice to prepare students for development of this ability, as only a qualified thesis will allow for complexity in argumentation. For this reason, a thesis formula with a qualification embedded in it, can help scaffold up to a qualified argument.

> **Time Commitment**
>
> "Argumentation is easy to teach when abbreviated and superficial, yet difficult to teach properly so that it is thoroughly and convincingly practiced by students. Additionally, it will usually manifest in longer responses such as at least one long paragraph, a full essay, or a document based question. Therefore, anticipating and budgeting an appropriate amount of time will become paramount to success for both students, in producing arguments, and teachers, in assessing argumentation. Yet, argumentation remains one of the most important transferable skills for lifelong success and must therefore be applied consistently to every other skill outlined in this manual, despite the time commitment and effort required."
>
> – Tillotson and Toms

When instructing on thesis building, a formula can also be helpful in supporting students who are working on pairing a claim with an appropriate line of reasoning to provide a full thesis. For each thesis variables are used as placeholders for the argument. "X" stands for a concession or counterpoint, and more advanced presentations can use the "X" as a qualification. The three groupings of evidence that comprise the line of reasoning are "A", "B", and "C". "Y" stands for the claim, or argument. Three examples of formulas would be:

1. "X, however, A, B, and C. Therefore Y."
2. "Although X, Y. This is evidenced by A, B, and C."
3. "Despite X, Y because A, B, and C."

It is sometimes easier for students to make a chart of the information they need to include as seen in the one below and on the next page:

Prompt and Skills Required				
Compare and contrast (c/c) the benefits (E) of applying for a part time job and joining marching band.				
Counterpoint, Qualification, or Negation	**Line of Reasoning**			**Claim**
X = Concession	A = Category 1	B = Category 2	C = Category 3	Y = Argument
Compromise time to work on academics	Getting a job makes you money but joining the marching band costs you money	Getting a job has you interacting with the public and your boss, but joining the marching band provides interaction with friends	Getting a job can end when you quit, but joining the band is for a whole school year.	They are similar in time commitment, but getting a job is more beneficial.
Completed thesis using "X, however A, B, and C. Therefore, Y."				
Student Response: *Both getting a job and joining the band take up a large portion of time, however, the financial consequences, social interactions, and length of commitment are all different. Therefore, getting a job is more beneficial.*				

Prompt and Skills Required				
Evaluate to what extent (E) the Second Great Awakening that occurred in the United States in the 19th century (c/x) led to (c/e) changes (CCOT) in American society.				
Counterpoint, Qualification, or Negation	**Line of Reasoning**			**Claim**
Religious movement, not a social movement	Enhanced roles women could play which upset men	Increased class conflict as the rich and middle class were swept up by it and the poor were not	Solidified political polarization around reform efforts that came from it	Did cause significant changes in society as it created an increase in social conflict through increased divisiveness
Completed thesis using "Although X, Y. This is evidenced by A, B, and C."				
Student Response: *Although the Second Great Awakening was a religious movement, it caused significant changes in society that transcended the religious domain, specifically that of increased divisiveness. This is evidenced by enhanced female participation, increased tension between classes, and strengthening and separation of political ideology.*				

While a thesis is an argument as it has both a claim and a line of reasoning, it is only a precursor to argumentation. Argumentation involves elaboration on the thesis, providing supporting details culled from the categories organized to form the line of reasoning. Thus, argumentation can only be exhibited, even in its most basic form, through a well-developed paragraph. The end goal should be to practice argumentation to eventually build long essays.

Argumentation in Basic Form

When first introducing basic argumentation, it may be helpful to employ shorter responses to begin with before expecting students to be able to write a long essay. Freshman and early secondary students will find this activity particularly helpful in practicing thesis elaboration especially if they are still feeling overwhelmed with the formatting of a long essay. In this way, students can learn how to perform argumentation without concerning themselves over differences between introductory and body paragraph structures or composition organization. When students are asked to answer a difficult question in only one paragraph it is easier for the teacher to diagnose, and the student to reflect on, basic mistakes made in argumentation. If written correctly, and the historical thinking skills are employed successfully, the students will achieve the same level of deep thinking, even if their answer to the prompt is limited to a single paragraph.

For students who struggle with organization of even a single paragraph, some scaffolding regarding sentence order could be helpful as seen below:

Argumentation in One Paragraph
1st Sentence: WHAT is your claim and line of reasoning: "Y because A, B, and C."   **2nd Sentence:** HOW does one key piece of evidence relate to A   **3rd Sentence:** WHY does A support your claim?   **4th Sentence:** HOW does one key piece of evidence relate to B   **5th Sentence:** WHY does B support your claim?   **6th Sentence:** HOW does one key piece of evidence relate to C   **7th Sentence:** WHY does C support your claim?

This one paragraph formula can eventually be amended and expanded to a five paragraph essay once proficiency in a single paragraph is achieved. Students actively developing argumentation in this basic form require narrative feedback, as it is crucial to student advancement through metacognition. Employing academic feedback language, as highlighted in Chapter 3, will help students isolate patterns in their writing allowing them to differentiate between progress being made and challenges yet to be overcome so they can advance to longer essays.

Argumentation in Advanced Form

Proficiency in the most complex form of argumentation culminates in transferability to medical journal submissions, doctoral dissertations, and closing arguments in court cases. In the social studies classroom, more advanced argumentation results in a three to five paragraph long essay, a document based question, or a research paper. When conducting a document based question or a research paper, the students should ensure that they analyze and cite sources, through an accepted citation procedure such as Chicago or APA, or even through in-text attribution as part of the provision of evidence. As a reminder, how to analyze a document for a document based question utilizing the historical thinking skills is outlined in Chapter 8: Interpretation.

When amending the basic argumentation paragraph outline to facilitate development of a long essay, context would be required in an introduction paragraph, followed by Sentence 1 as a thesis. Sentences 2-3 make up the topic sentence of the 1st body paragraph, and the rest of the formula would finish the other topic sentences in the same way. The rest of each body paragraph itself should be one or two iterations of the conclusions they drew written for a skill in conjunction with elaboration of additional evidence. The last sentence or two of the body paragraphs should focus on reiterating how the evidence provided proves the claim from the thesis statement and thus ties the argument back to the prompt. Finally, a concluding paragraph could include a rewording of the thesis and provide an opportunity to highlight innovative synthesis if appropriate.

Troubleshooting

Student Misconception #1: Misinterpreting the question asked

Diagnosing questions is the most prevalent obstacle for student success when it comes to showing mastery of any skill. Too often students will write a very proficient off-topic essay answering a question that was never asked. Therein lies the challenge for the stalwart instructor determined to teach a refined understanding of critical thinking skills.

Using synonyms to help students reword the prompt can be helpful in clarifying what task a question is asking the student to perform. It is sometimes necessary to highlight during a whole group debrief of a class exercise, even a word as simple as a preposition in a prompt. In overlooking even one word, a student can answer the wrong question, as "in" has a very different meaning from "of". Particularly, students may need assistance highlighting the topics and skills of the essay, as well as focusing on what the prompt is asking from them as they analyze.

In the example used throughout this chapter of the Second Great Awakening, many common student pitfalls may occur in diagnosing the prompt and analyzing the evidence. They may become hyper-focused on the changes developing from the Industrial Revolution and overlook the fact that those changes have to be connected to social interactions for this prompt. It might be important to remind students of the parameters of the prompt, for example, a teacher may need to remind the students that the prompt about the Great Awakening is asking about society, not economics. Also, students may focus too much on what they learned in class about the reform movements that came from the Second Great Awakening, but the prompt requires a discussion of social interactions. To develop the ability to see nuance in prompts requires copious exposure, practice, and feedback.

Student Misconception #2: Disregarding the order of the steps

To arrive at a finished product of merit, there are several steps in critical thinking that need to be conducted, and they need to be applied in order. There is a risk of students working out of order when they are learning argumentation, which will make their analysis and writing much more difficult to complete well. Students have preconceived notions about argumentation from earlier exposure to this activity. Often, they develop the idea that the argument starts with the claim. However, the claim should only be made after properly evaluating context and evidence. This needs to be clarified through direct instruction. By skipping the thinking process that would allow them to arrive at a valid claim and provide an accurate line of reasoning, students often end up submitting only partially complete or indefensible thesis statements. It can help to review the steps that need to be completed in order to arrive at a well-reasoned thesis statement. To address this issue, remind students that starting with the claim is less productive because it will end up narrowing their ability to leverage evidence supporting the claim they assumed rather than deduced. An anchor chart can be helpful in outlining the steps to remind students of the order in which thinking tasks must be performed for effective argumentation:

Mandatory Pre-Work Before Writing

1. Analyze what the prompt is asking you to do by figuring out which skills, topics, and time periods are involved
2. Brainstorm all you know about the topic by writing down specific people, events, and phenomena within the context of the prompt
3. Gather and analyze evidence or research in terms of the question asked
4. Create a line of reasoning by grouping the research into categories of evidence
5. Create a claim by merging conclusions about the groupings of the research
6. Build a concession by deciding which argument you *won't* make based on groupings of evidence
7. Write a first draft of a thesis statement

Student Misconception #3: Repeating unsuccessful attempts and expecting change

Much of a student's experience in formal education focuses on repetition and practice. Therefore, too often a student will be under the impression that if they simply complete enough writing attempts they will get better at it. However, the students must learn that their writing will get better only if they apply the feedback that the teacher has given. One component for improvement is indeed providing narrative feedback to students. Yet, the more often overlooked contributor involves teaching students to look for patterns in feedback, problem solving their missteps, and application of corrective measures. Utilizing a structured feedback language, as shown in Chapter 3, will help students see such patterns and learn how to self-correct. Metacognitive practices need to be overtly and purposefully included in teaching the skill of argumentation to improve in these areas. With these metacognitive practices in place, students can see change over time in their ability to argue more successfully.

Importance of Argumentation

In isolation, the historical thinking skills allow students to manipulate and analyze history and information. However, in isolation the skills are used only for limited purposes. In order for a student to fully express to another person how they arrived at their conclusions or claims, they must be able to argue. Once the students become proficient in argumentation, they will have the skills to explain abstract thinking and persuade others. For this reason, it is imperative that quality argumentation is taught at the high school level so that students are prepared for a world based on the exchange and adoption of ideas. Argumentation is deeply embedded in college writing as well as being a basic requirement in the career world. Students must be able to advocate for their thoughts and themselves through purposefully constructed arguments, whether it be in a job interview or with loved ones. The historical thinking skills help the students to think, but argumentation helps the students to express what they thought and is thus, in some ways, even more important.

Argumentation Reflection

Although this skill may seem the most familiar it decidedly takes the most time to practice and assess. Here are some metacognitive questions to get started with reflection:

1. How has your understanding of argumentation changed after reading this chapter?

2. How will the argumentation skill serve students in their adult lives?

3. Where do you anticipate your students having the most misunderstandings and what scaffolding will they need when introduced to the skill?

4. What steps do you need to take to increase your confidence in grading argumentation?

Chapter 12:

Classroom Implementation

Maintaining Rigor

One of the greatest challenges associated with shifting to skills-based teaching is maintaining high expectations. Teachers' and students' expectations for success have to shift from immediate results on any one measure, to that of long-term changes in metacognition about behaviors and transfer goals associated with critical thinking. Skill advancement will be inconsistent, but long term. Students will face and express repeated frustrations as they begin to develop the perseverance required to exhibit critical thinking skills. Students who enroll in a skills-based course are going to need to realign their definition of success with a growth mindset. This will allow long term changes in habits of mind where improvements are assessed in consistency as opposed to on singular examples. To this end, teachers have to offer consistent rigor, clarity of instruction, and maintain the high standard set at the beginning of the year.

Frankly, the solution to rigor lies in the teacher's determination to maintain it. The reality is that the only way this historical thinking skills system works is if the teacher wants to do it, wants to do it well, and has a support system. The historical thinking skills can be difficult to differentiate, learn, implement, and teach. Yet the payoff is worth it; the students will leave the classroom better thinkers. If the teacher maintains and teaches grit, implements a flexible skill focused approach, and overcomes naysayers, the classroom will evolve into a growth focused community of historical investigators.

Maintaining rigorous expectations high enough that students actually have to grow their skills to reach a point of success is decidedly the hardest thing a skills teacher has to face. When looking into the face of a discouraged student, even the most dedicated teacher can feel self-doubt about the systemic changes implemented, particularly if the student

Student Engagement

"The first year of implementing the historical thinking skills I found that my class got 'harder' according to my students. The reality is, it did! Instead of focusing on a student's ability to recall information, they were asked to use their abstract thinking skills every day. As a mantra, I tell my students, whenever they are struggling, 'If your brain doesn't hurt, you're not doing it right.' Tillotson tells her students, 'When you are doing history right, 80% is thinking, and 20% is writing down what your brain did.' Eventually my students recognize the struggle of abstract thinking as the good work of a historian, not a sign of incompetency. However, the reality is that teenagers are not always hard workers in the face of failure, do not want to do the hard work, or have external concerns that take precedence over developing critical thinking in my classroom. If the students don't choose to learn the information, there is no way they can apply it in abstract thinking. Despite my best efforts, not every student will become masters in their historical craft by the end of the school year, but MORE of them will than if I used a traditional content approach. That is what encourages me to maintain a rigorous classroom when students don't do their homework or resist the hard work. One issue I do not have is students not liking history or being bored. They may not want to do the work, but they are engaged and challenged every day. Some even acknowledge that history doesn't seem as bad as they used to think it was, which might be the real victory."

– Toms

normally performs well. These situations can incite feelings of a need to simplify or create successes that the student has not actually achieved, just so that a success can be celebrated. However, continuously placating students who cannot reach a rigorous expectation only serves to limit their growth and instill false confidence. The solution is to scaffold the skills, teach a growth mindset, and learn each student's individual needs so that helpful and accurate feedback can be utilized and appropriate scaffolding can be implemented. As with anything new, the first year of implementation is the most difficult. Yet, once success is demonstrated by students toward the end of the first year, the next year of instruction will be easier because the end result can be used to leverage previous successes and stay the course.

Planning in a Skills Based Classroom

When planning in a skills based classroom, backwards planning is essential. One must begin with understanding how the skills will manifest in the lesson and build the expectations of performance so that the rigor is met. Asking students to perform skills will provide not only breadth, but depth. The mindset and culture of the class must focus on achieving critical thinking as transfer goals, rather than simple completion or basic compliance which many teachers and students seem to default to in times of stress.

It is critical for the teacher focused on supporting students' growth to show vulnerability in their attempts at a new skill in their profession. When planning lessons, much of what is experienced by both the teachers and the students will necessarily be first attempts. These often come with mixed results including successes and learning opportunities for teachers and students alike. Being transparent with students about nascent attempts at developing new lessons with new formats is critical in building rapport and ethos with students. When being vulnerable and transparent in this way, we found that having a team of like-minded individuals made the less successful early attempts to maintain rigor easier to digest and learn from. In addition, working with peers offered invaluable support in maintaining morale throughout this trying period in the history of education.

Create a Team of Like-Minded Teachers

Create a support team of like-minded individuals who are also struggling with the noble challenge of teaching critical thinking. This then allows for collaboration, moral support, and an infusion of determination at the moments when it is most needed. Collaboration will be intrinsic to the teacher's practice of metacognition in their own skill development and so cannot be underestimated in its significance. Using comparisons of experiences and leveraging different points of view from multiple teachers will allow each teacher on the team to delve deeper into the skills to allow for greater self-knowledge to then model and disseminate. Feeling alone and occasionally perceiving that one's efforts are futile will happen to even the most dedicated teachers. Yet, frequent validations from a team regarding the difficulties of maintaining rigor, but the necessity of doing so, are essential in sustaining dedication to this challenging shift in mindset. As a team of educators develop more acumen within that team of critical thinking skills teachers, the load will become more bearable.

One of the benefits of creating a team of educators to implement the skills system is to enhance opportunities for

Understanding Ourselves

"When we set out to write this book, it never occurred to us we were embarking on such an amazing journey of self-discovery thanks to the skills. Throughout the process of writing each chapter, not only did we develop more nuanced understandings of each skill, even after years of employing this system, but we were able to make powerful and redefining observations about our own thinking processes. We knew early on that having a big picture thinker paired with a detail-oriented thinker was a surefire way to explore the methodologies outlined in the book. But the benefits of employing the skills to write the skills book far exceeded our expectations. By using the interpretation skills, we were able to try on the partner's thinking style, experiment with new methods of articulating metacognition, and gain new teaching strategies to employ with all our future students. I wish I were able to capture what happened for both of us over the course of this writing, but I can say definitively that much of our conversation while writing centered around how each of us was processing information, how each employed the skills, and how we could use this newfound understanding to enhance our practice in the future. This then is another benefit of like-minded individuals: the opportunity for discourse and collaboration to enhance your own self-actualization."

– Tillotson

vertical alignment. The historical thinking skills are so difficult for students that while some success will be seen in the first year, students will not be able to master all of the skills in one academic year. Indeed, true comprehensive mastery of a skills-based system is only possible through repeated exposure and focus across the grade levels. The team of like-minded individuals will allow for continuity across grades in secondary education, providing more likelihood of success in transferring the goals beyond the classroom. In this way, systemic change takes place not just within the social studies classroom, but throughout the social studies department.

This approach to education is so revolutionary that it would be difficult to mandate it as a system on a larger scale in one fell swoop. Teachers have to be the agents of this systemic revolution and need to understand the importance of consistency in application in order to maintain fidelity in implementation. If teachers are given agency to support one another, and consistently employ this and other supporting resources, the theories and methodology in this work can revolutionize any school district regardless of scope or size. If a district wants to adopt these strategic modifications en masse, teacher buy-in has to be established at the beginning of implementation and must be organic, not mandated, for success in implementation of skills focused learning.

Managing Stakeholders

One of the key components to success in transitioning to a skills focus system is to manage expectations for all stakeholders including instructors themselves, students, administrators, and parents. It needs to be communicated early and often that skills-based learning is a lengthy process which takes time to not only implement, but to see any measurable results. It is important for teachers adopting this system to be aware, and communicate to parents, that students will not exhibit tremendous levels of success on the initial exercises with any one skill. Only over the course of much practice and active spiral teaching will progress be made.

Expectations should be communicated to the students in an overt manner, managing expectations even as early as introducing typical timelines for progress on the syllabus. Parents need to be introduced to the longevity of progress in a skills-based system through communication not just from the student, but from the teacher as well. Parent communication can take the form of a newsletter explaining how skills-based learning differs from content focused learning, open house announcements, and letters home just before report cards are issued to help parents manage their expectations.

The reality is, often true growth will not manifest until the second semester. If done correctly, the students' grades should get higher over the course of the year, not stay stagnant. Teachers should frequently offer narrative feedback. If consistently offered, students will increase their responsiveness to feedback, and they will see incremental growth. However, recordable progress for data collection, like that needed for report cards, will take weeks to accumulate and months to see progress. Administrators need to be prepared for changes that will take longer to appear in the gradebook and that may take longer to manifest and be reported through progress checks and report cards. To offer support for stakeholders to practice patience and await large and consistent improvement, student samples can be used to validate growth over time and assessment of current skill mastery.

Epiphanies

"Despite years of practice, we found that even as we wrote this book, we continued to refine our understanding of each of the skills. We found ourselves discussing for extended periods of time how each of the skills manifest in our classrooms, and from there discovered new layers and nuance regarding the nature of each skill. The more we discussed and dissected the skills to articulate them for this work, the more we discovered how the skills intersect and these intersections create dependency on early skills in order to develop later skills. What surprised us was that we had already spent years teaching the skills, thinking about the skills, and talking about the skills. Yet it was not until we had to sit down and write it out with one focused argument that an even deeper understanding developed for us to record. It was a stark reminder to never be too confident with the skills and to expect continued refinement in understanding through metacognition."

– Toms and Tillotson

Final Thoughts

Despite the difficulties associated with implementation of a skills focused system, the ultimate transfer goals of critical thinking are worth the perseverance. Productive members of society must be able to demonstrate proficiency in critical thinking. Focused instruction on causation, comparison, contextualization, change and continuity over time, interpretation, evaluation, and synthesis will push students to not only develop a growth mindset, but also process their world accurately and thoughtfully.

Given the google-able nature of the world in the 21st century, it is more important than ever for students to be able to leverage their thinking skills to originate thoughts. The ultimate goals of innovative synthesis and argumentation to achieve adoption of new ideas will allow students to be competitive in an increasingly globalized world and allow them to bring valuable and creative solutions to tomorrow's problems. To make this vision a reality, teachers need to recognize their role in creating thinkers and the easiest method to foster a critical thinking environment is shifting to a skills based approach.

Afterword

During the unusual teaching required during the COVID-19 pandemic we found that the foundation we had built with the historical thinking skills provided a bedrock for instruction that anchored students, provided familiarity and allowed for continuity of rigorous instruction regardless of locale or quantity of live interaction each student experienced. The vertical alignment of skill-focused instruction not only provided clarity in curriculum but allowed for a more comfortable transition for students in the fall of 2020 to a new subject and teacher when so many other circumstances in their life could not be described as "normal".

In order to provide student perspectives about how skills based instruction works in a virtual environment, we conducted a survey to share with readers invested in providing the optimal opportunity to their students despite the challenges of 2020 and beyond. Between December 14th and 18th, 2020 we conducted an anonymous student survey of over 200 participants from five different teachers who have fully implemented this historical thinking skills system in their classrooms. At the end of the first full fall semester of virtual learning, students reported a variety of valuable information from which can be gleaned opportunities to enhance education in the coming years. In some ways, there were aspects of virtual learning that the students found to be helpful, including the ability to rewatch recordings of lectures, extended time on assignments, ability to thoroughly research before writing, having all their assignments and notes organized for them in one place and being in the comfort of home while completing assignments.

When asked which skills students felt they had improved competence in based on work completed during the fall semester, over 60% of students suggested causation, comparison, and contextualization were already showing signs of strengthening after only five months. The reasons for this success, as self-reported by the students, was attributed to:

- direct instruction with focus on the skills and skills workshops
- practice opportunities with writing including short answer questions
- document analysis, long essays, and thesis writing

- individualized narrative feedback and tutoring from their instructors
- highlighted relevancy of real-life application of the skills
- opportunities to correct their writing based on teacher feedback
- sentence stems for skill development
- skill focused review activities, mastery assessments, warm-ups, and exit tickets

While 50% or more suggested they felt the need for more support with interpretation, evaluation and synthesis, these challenges were attributed to:

- these particular skills being harder to master as they are more complex
- not being able to differentiate between these skills and the simpler building block skills used to perform them
- insufficient practice as the school year had only been four months long at this point in time
- a general struggle with distance learning and the stress of the COVID-19 pandemic.

This supports the contention that even in Upper Bloom's there are levels of complexity when it comes to exhibition of skill proficiency with some skills needing more time to develop, and thus requiring more repetition of instruction and more numerous practice opportunities. Yet, by necessity, these more advanced skills cannot be performed reliably until those building blocks are themselves embedded as ways of thinking, organizing information, and approaching tasks assigned since so many of the building block skills are embedded in the more advanced skills of interpretation, evaluation and synthesis.

When asked which processes facilitated the most growth in skills over the course of the semester, the majority of students were able to articulate that the most beneficial exercises were specifically:

- interactive notebooks
- evaluative ranking projects
- research assignments
- modified debates
- Socratic seminars
- opportunities to interact with peers
- application of skills to real world current events articles and discussions
- having the ability to make a choice in product delivery
- writing exercises

Additionally, one can see how each of these activities lends itself to, and is enhanced by, a skills based focus.

Interestingly, over 40% of student respondents reported that they were more confident in their writing abilities by rating their growth from the previous year at a 7 or 8 on a scale of 1-10. This strongly indicates that the vertical alignment provided in our AP Social Studies department on the skills and argumentation help the students to grow, rather than regress, even in times of extenuating circumstances. And most astonishingly, over 70% of students reported that they were consciously aware of using the skills from social studies outside of the classroom in other subjects or even in their daily lives at least once a week or more, with over 25% reporting they saw themselves using social studies skills outside of the classroom daily or more than once a day. Given that this is the focus of a skills based classroom, this self-reporting provides ample evidence that a skills based and metacognitive focus can indeed transcend traditional classroom structures.

In general, patterns that emerged in assessing the narrative data from over 200 participants in this survey showed that while virtual learning did generate challenges for students compared to traditional classroom learning, they were still able to articulate the benefits they saw for themselves in growing their skill abilities and enhancing the transferability of their critical thinking skills even in the most trying of times. This is one of the many reasons we believe skills based learning is destined to evolve the social studies discipline and become the working standard in the 21st century.

Reproducibles

Reproducibles referenced in this manual can be found on the following pages in the order listed below. They may be copied for school use only.

- Lower Blooms Common Task Verbs
- Upper Blooms Common Task Verbs

- What does my feedback mean?

- Skills-at-a-Glance

- Causation (c/e) Anchor Chart
- Comparison (c/c) Anchor Chart
- Contextualization (c/x) Anchor Chart
- Change and Continuity over Time (CCOT) Anchor Chart
- Interpretation (I) Anchor Chart
- Evaluation (E) Anchor Chart
- Synthesis (S) Anchor Chart
- Argumentation Anchor Chart

Lower Blooms Common Task Verbs

Different skills require different tasks. Questions may call for <u>more than one task</u>, such as both to identify and explain. Some tasks are more complex than others. For example, composing a list may only require a complete sentence, but one may need to write several paragraphs for a satisfactory discussion, including well-developed examples as support, in order to adequately explain some phenomenon.

List/Identify: Listing or identifying is a task that requires no more than a <u>simple enumeration</u> of some factors or characteristics. A list <u>does not require any</u> causal <u>explanations</u>.

- ***To Tie a Shoe***: *Items required include shoes, holes in the shoe for laces, and shoelaces*
- ***In History Class:*** *You might be asked to list or identify three characteristics Presidents consider when making appointments, so one might include party, race, gender, etc.*

Define: A definition requires you to <u>provide a meaning</u> for a word or concept. <u>Examples may help</u> to demonstrate understanding of the definition.

- ***To Tie a Shoe***: *Is to tighten a shoe around one's foot so the shoe is not easily removed.*
- ***In History Class:*** *You may be instructed to write what the Presidential cabinet is in your own words.*

Describe: A description involves providing a <u>depiction or portrayal</u> of a phenomenon or its most significant characteristics. Descriptions most often address "what" questions.

- ***To Tie a Shoe***: *Pulling together and securing of the laces with a tie or bow as a closure.*
- ***In History Class:*** *You may be asked to describe reasons for the decline in voter turnout, in the description you must do <u>more than simply list facts</u>—you must actually describe the reasons. For example, you may describe that the expansion of suffrage <u>led to</u> a decline in overall voter turnout because once voting was made available to more individuals, the overall percentage of those voting declined.*

Discuss: Discussions generally require that you <u>explore relationships</u> between different concepts or phenomena. Identifying, describing, and explaining could be required tasks involved in writing a satisfactory discussion.

- ***To Tie a Shoe***: *Not all shoes lace; shoes not "required" to stay on might not have them.*
- ***In History Class:*** *Do application level thinking, for example, a discussion prompt might require you to differentiate between demographic characteristics and how they align with the two primary political ideologies.*

Upper Blooms Common Task Verbs

Explain: An explanation involves the exploration of <u>possible causal relationships</u>. When providing explanations, you should identify and discuss <u>logical connections or causal patterns</u> that exist between or among various phenomena.

- ***To Tie a Shoe***: *Take one lace in each hand, cross laces, and tuck lace A under lace B...*
- ***In History Class***: *You need to record the critical thinking that you performed in a coherent way.*

Analyze: This task usually requires <u>separating</u> a phenomenon into its component parts or characteristics as a <u>way of understanding the whole</u>. An analysis should yield explicit conclusions that are explained or supported by specific evidence and/or well-reasoned arguments.

- ***To Tie a Shoe***: *A child will be less proficient at tying shoes than an adult due to 1) a lack of coordination in fine motor skills, 2) fewer years of practice and experience, 3) a lack of motivation as a result of inexperience with causes/effects of tripping and injury.*
- ***In History Class***: *Do the causation, comparison, contextualization, interpretation, and/or change and continuity over time skill.*

Compare/Contrast: This task requires you to make specific links between two or more concepts or phenomena. You should understand that it is important to note <u>similarities AND differences</u> between the concepts or phenomena under consideration.

- ***To Tie a Shoe***: *Wet shoelaces might be harder to untie than dry shoelaces.*
- ***In History Class***: *Do the comparison skill.*

Evaluate/Assess: An evaluation or assessment involves considering <u>how well something meets a certain standard</u>, and as such, generally requires a thesis. It is important to identify the criteria used in the evaluation. If no criteria are explicitly given in the question, you should take care to clearly identify the ones that you choose to employ. Specific examples may be applied to the criteria to support your thesis. Evaluation or assessment requires explicit connections between the thesis or argument and the supporting evidence.

- ***To Tie a Shoe***: *Shoes with laces are MORE appropriate for gym classes than shoes without laces i.e., 1) tend to come with better grip on the outer sole, 2) better safety/security at higher speeds and levels of activity, 3) enhanced confidence leading to better performance in athletic events*
- ***In History Class***: *Answer an evaluation prompt or answer a "To what extent" prompt.*

What does my feedback mean?

Vague/Example? - You need to add specific examples and evidence.
  Vague: America is free.
  Specific/Not vague: America ensures inalienable rights **such as** life, liberty, and the pursuit of happiness.

Connect ideas- You need to put the two ideas together in one sentence to argue a point.
  Not connected: America is dramatic in elections. There was one in 2016.
  Connected: America is dramatic in elections, **as seen in** the presidential election of 2016.

Does not support argument- You need better evidence to support your response to the prompt *or* change your argument.
  Does not support argument: America is awesome because we fight lots of wars.
  Supports argument: America is awesome because there is free K-12 education.
  OR America sometimes makes bad choices by fighting too many wars.

Does not answer/argue/reference prompt- The evidence you provided is not on the topic of the prompt. You are missing the connection to the prompt.
  Does not respond to prompt:
  Prompt: Has America's economy crashed?
  Answer: The Cold War was against the USSR. (evidence is off theme and topic and it doesn't mention economy)
  Responds to prompt: Answer: America's economy crashed in the Great Depression.

So what?/Finish your thought - Why is this important? What is the significance? Why does the idea matter? How does it connect to the prompt?
  Lacks the "so what": America is a representative democracy.
  Has the "so what": America is a representative democracy, **so** the government is designed to reflect what the people want through representation and voting.

Incomplete sentence- You are either missing the subject or object of your sentence so it doesn't make sense or answer the prompt completely.
  Incomplete Sentence: Because it helps the economy. (What does?? IDK!)
  Complete Sentence: America builds infrastructure **because** it helps the economy.

Confusing - I could not understand your grammar or reasoning. Start over.

Not quite/not really- Response is very problematic and probably historically inaccurate. Start over.

Causation (c/e)

Student can discern whether causes or effects are being assessed in a prompt and accurately respond, isolating causes from and connecting causes to processes and effects.

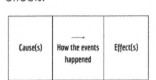

Cause(s)	How the events happened →	Effect(s)

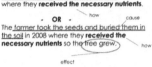

Example:

The apple tree grew *(effect)* because the farmer took the seeds and buried them in the soil in 2008 *(cause)* where they **received the necessary nutrients** *(how)*.

- OR -

The farmer took the seeds and buried them in the soil in 2008 where they **received the necessary nutrients** *(cause)* so the tree grew *(effect)* *(how)*.

Comparison (c/c)

Student can discern that comparison is being assessed in a prompt and accurately respond by isolating and describing similarities and differences.

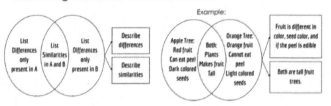

Example:

Apple Tree: Red fruit, Can eat peel, Dark colored seeds. Both: Plants, Makes fruit, Tall. Orange Tree: Orange fruit, Cannot eat peel, Light colored seeds.

Fruit is different in color, seed color, and if the peel is edible. Both are tall fruit trees.

Contextualization (c/x)

Student can discern that contextualization is being assessed and accurately respond by generating and connecting relevant details and themes to the subject.

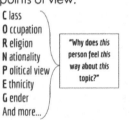

What was happening just before or during the topic? What big themes are present? Be specific with details!

How does the context connect to the topic? What is the significance? Why is this important to know?

Topic you are studying

Example:

The apple tree was in the fifth row of a large apple orchard. It was well cared for by John Doe, the wealthy owner of the orchard, so it was able to survive the devastating drought in 2015 that killed the northern neighbor's lone apple tree.

(apple tree that survived and fruited)

Change and Continuity Over Time (CCOT)

Student can discern that continuities and changes over time are being assessed and accurately respond by isolating and describing these patterns. Student can differentiate between continuities and changes over time within and across time periods.

Circumstances present before the development	A turning point or a series of factors and how it led to a development	Characteristics that exist after the development
Characteristics that stayed the same over a specific period of time or across time periods		

Example:

Due to a completed maturation, the apple tree started to produce apples. *(change)* Despite completed maturation, the apple tree kept growing taller. *(continuity)*

Interpretation (I)

Student can discern that interpretation is being assessed, and can isolate contributing factors to various points of view.

C lass
O ccupation
R eligion
N ationality
P olitical view
E thnicity
G ender
And more...

"Why does *this* person feel *this* way about *this* topic?"

Example: What explains John Doe's reaction to changes in the stock market?

Step 1:
C - Middle
O - Farmer
R - Baptist
N - American
P - Republican
E - Caucasian
G - Male

Step 2:
→ Not affluent, must plan for retirement savings
→ Knows about fluctuations in crop prices
→ Concerned about free market economic policies

Step 3: As a Republican middle class farmer, John Doe fears fluctuation of the stock market in commodity price changes because he wants to ensure he maximizes crop sales and retirement savings based on free market trends.

Evaluation (E)

Student can discern that evaluation is being assessed, can appropriately weigh and choose between potential arguments, events and ideas that relate to the assigned task.

Weigh evidence then choose:
- Option 1: Collaboration (Yes) — The evidence supports...
- Option 2: Contradiction (No) — The evidence does not support...
- Option 3: Qualification (Sometimes) — The evidence supports, BUT...

Example:
- A graph shows that orange trees grow better in warm climates like Florida.
- Orange trees planted in Michigan have died because of the winters.
- There is not enough natural rainfall in desert climates to provide enough water to keep an orange tree healthy.

After weighing these facts, the evidence supports the argument that it is likely a good idea to plant orange trees in Florida.

Synthesis (S)

Student can discern that synthesis is being assessed, and can make connections between a given issue and related developments in a different context.

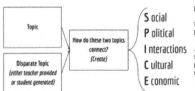

Topic → How do these two topics connect? (Create) ← Disparate Topic (either teacher provided or student generated)

S ocial
P olitical
I nteractions
C ultural
E conomic

Example:

Topic: John Doe and his apple tree
Disparate Topic: an otter and its pup

John Doe tends to his apple tree in the same way that an otter tends to her pup. Both have a dependent they feed, monitor, and protect from harm.

Argumentation

The student can articulate a defensible claim in the form of a clear and compelling thesis that evaluates the importance of multiple factors and can support the argument through close analysis and use of relevant and diverse evidence, framing the argument and evidence around a thinking skill.

Option 1: Contradiction
Option 2: Collaboration
Option 3: Qualification
Thesis (claim)

Line of Reasoning
Reason 1 → Specific historical evidence for all parts of the HTS
Reason 2 → Specific historical evidence for all parts of the HTS
Reason 3 → Specific historical evidence for all parts of the HTS

Example: Although X, Y. This is evidenced by A, B, and C.

While orange trees can grow in other states, it is likely a good idea to plant orange trees in Florida. This is evidenced by Florida's sufficient natural rainfall to support the growth of orange trees, its consistent year round sunlight to encourage tree growth, and its nutrient rich soil to facilitate fruit production.

Causation (c/e)

Student can discern whether causes or effects are being assessed in a prompt and accurately respond, isolating causes from and connecting causes to processes and effects.

Cause(s)	How the events happened	Effect(s)
	→	

Example:

The apple tree grew because the farmer took the seeds and buried them in the soil in 2008 where they **received the necessary nutrients.**

effect   how   cause

- OR -

The farmer took the seeds and buried them in the soil in 2008 where they **received the necessary nutrients** so the tree grew.

cause   how   effect

Comparison (C/C)

Student can discern that comparison is being assessed in a prompt and accurately respond by isolating and describing similarities and differences.

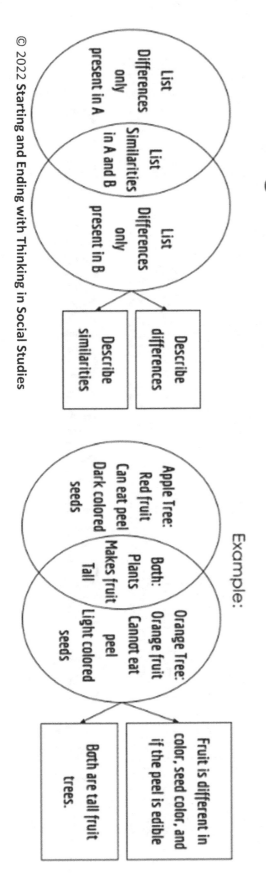

List Differences only present in A

List Similarities in A and B

List Differences only present in B

Describe differences

Describe similarities

Example:

Apple Tree:
Red fruit
Can eat peel
Dark colored seeds

Both:
Plants
Makes fruit
Tall

Orange Tree:
Orange fruit
Cannot eat peel
Light colored seeds

Fruit is different in color, seed color, and if the peel is edible

Both are tall fruit trees.

Contextualization (c/x)

Student can discern that contextualization is being assessed and accurately respond by generating and connecting relevant details and themes to the subject.

What was happening just before or during the topic?
What big themes are present? Be specific with details!

Example:

How does the context connect to the topic? What is the significance? Why is this important to know?

The apple tree was in the fifth row of a large apple orchard. It was well cared for by John Doe, the wealthy owner of the orchard, so it was able to survive the devastating drought in 2015 that killed the northern neighbor's lone apple tree.

Topic you are studying

(apple tree that survived and fruited)

Change and Continuity Over Time (CCOT)

Student can discern that continuities and changes over time are being assessed and accurately respond by isolating and describing these patterns. Student can differentiate between continuities and changes over time within and across time periods.

Circumstances present before the development	A turning point or a series of factors and *how* it led to a development	Characteristics that exist after the development
Characteristics that stayed the same over a specific period of time or across time periods		

Example:
Due to a completed maturation, the apple tree started to produce apples. — change
Despite completed maturation, the apple tree kept growing taller. — continuity

Interpretation (I)

Student can discern that interpretation is being assessed, and can isolate contributing factors to various points of view.

C lass
O ccupation
R eligion
N ationality
P olitical view
E thnicity
G ender
And more...

"Why does this person feel *this* way about *this* topic?"

Example: What explains John Doe's reaction to changes in the stock market?

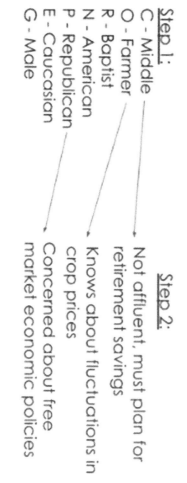

Step 1:
C - Middle
O - Farmer
R - Baptist
N - American
P - Republican
E - Caucasian
G - Male

Step 2:
Not affluent, must plan for retirement savings

Knows about fluctuations in crop prices

Concerned about free market economic policies

Step 3: As a Republican middle class farmer, John Doe fears fluctuation of the stock market in commodity price changes because he wants to ensure he maximizes crop sales and retirement savings based on free market trends.

Evaluation (E)

Student can discern that evaluation is being assessed, can appropriately weigh and choose between potential arguments, events and ideas that relate to the assigned task.

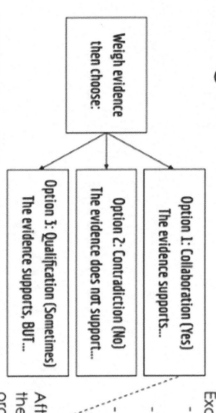

Weigh evidence then choose:

Option 1: Collaboration (Yes)
The evidence supports...

Option 2: Contradiction (No)
The evidence does not support....

Option 3: Qualification (Sometimes)
The evidence supports, BUT...

Example:
- A graph shows that orange trees grow better in warm climates like Florida.
- Orange trees planted in Michigan have died because of the winters.
- There is not enough natural rainfall in desert climates to provide enough water to keep an orange tree healthy.

After weighing these facts, the evidence supports the argument that it is likely a good idea to plant orange trees in Florida.

Synthesis (S)

Student can discern that synthesis is being assessed, and can make connections between a given issue and related developments in a different context.

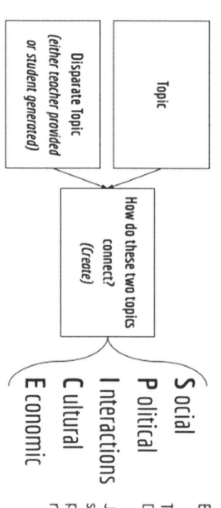

Topic

How do these two topics connect? (Create)

Disparate Topic (either teacher provided or student generated)

S ocial
P olitical
I nteractions
C ultural
E conomic

Example:

Topic: John Doe and his apple tree
Disparate Topic: an otter and its pup

John Doe tends to his apple tree in the same way that an otter tends to her pup. Both have a dependent they feed, monitor, and protect from harm.

Argumentation

The student can articulate a defensible claim in the form of a clear and compelling thesis that evaluates the importance of multiple factors and can support the argument through close analysis and use of relevant and diverse evidence, framing the argument and evidence around a thinking skill.

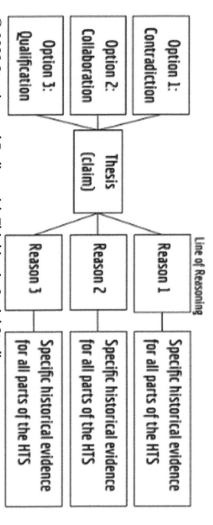

Line of Reasoning

| Option 1: Contradiction |
| Option 2: Collaboration |
| Option 3: Qualification |

Thesis (claim)

Reason 1	Specific historical evidence for all parts of the HTS
Reason 2	Specific historical evidence for all parts of the HTS
Reason 3	Specific historical evidence for all parts of the HTS

Example: *Although X, Y. This is evidenced by A, B, and C.*

While orange trees can grow in other states, it is likely a good idea to plant orange trees in Florida. This is evidenced by Florida's sufficient natural rainfall to support the growth of orange trees, its consistent year round sunlight to encourage tree growth, and its nutrient rich soil to facilitate fruit production.

Notes

-

References

Anderson, L., Krathwohl, D., eds. (2001). *A Taxonomy for Learning, Teaching, and Assessing: A Revision of Bloom's Taxonomy of Educational Objectives*. New York: Longman.

Bloom, B. S., Engelhart, M. D., First, E. J., Hill, W. H., Krathwohl, D. R. (1956). *Taxonomy of Educational Objects: The Classification of Educational Goals, Handbook I: Cognitive Domain*. New York: David McKay Company.

Dweck, C. (2006). *Mindset: The New Psychology of Success*. New York: Ballantine Books.

Hattie, J. (2012). *Visible Learning for Teachers: Maximizing impact on learning*. New York, NY: Routledge.

Lesh, B. (2011). *"Why Won't You Just Tell Us the Answer?": Teaching Historical Thinking in Grades 7-12*. Portland, Maine: Stenhouse Publishers.

Marzano, R. (2010). *Formative Assessment and Standards-Based Grading*. Bloomington, IN: Marzano Research Laboratory.

Marzano, R. (2019a). *The Handbook for the New Art and Science of Teaching*. Bloomington, IN: Solution Tree Press and ASCD.

Marzano, R. (2019b). *Understanding Rigor in the Classroom*. West Palm Beach, FL: Learning Sciences International.

Marzano, R. & Toth, M. (2013). *Deliberate practice for deliberate growth: Teacher evaluation systems for continuous instructional improvement.* West Palm Beach, FL: Learning Sciences International.

Silver, H., Strong, R., & Perini, M. (2007). *The Strategic Teacher: Selecting the Right Research-Based Strategy for Every Lesson*. Alexandria, VA: ASCD.

Wiggins, G., & McTighe, J. (2011). *The Understanding by Design Guide to Creating High-Quality Units*. Alexandria, VA: ASCD.

Acknowledgements

We would first like to thank Courtney Kunath who read each chapter as we wrote, to help us articulate the essence of this advanced use of historical thinking skills which she helped pilot at our school. She not only offered valuable feedback in finalizing this published work but also walked with us every day for years to refine the system with real students in real classrooms.

This book would not be possible without Shane McKay, who's trust in his teachers and vision of progressive education gave us the venue to experiment with a growth-mindset-grounded grading system, historical thinking skills as the focus of the classroom, and the nature of the social studies discipline in a public school setting.

Many thanks go to Rodger Tillotson who made us laugh every Saturday morning.

We simply could not have finished this ambitious project without the support of our fathers. Rob Toms offered his valuable time and fresh perspective reading every word of every page with his litigator's eye for detail. Ken Raftery was an invaluable source of encouragement as he continued to believe that Theresa could actually write a book.

Finally, we would like to thank the hundreds of students that passed through our classrooms, who had patience with us as we attempted to articulate the skills to them in the early years. Their questions, pushback, misunderstandings, patience, and honesty helped to refine our understanding and drove us to further differentiate, articulate more clearly, clarify relevance, and grow confidence in our system as we saw success after success.

Thank you one and all who contributed in their own ways.

About the Authors

Theresa Tillotson has a Bachelor of Science in Education from Bowling Green State University in Ohio and a Master of Arts in Political Science from the University of Texas at San Antonio. She has been teaching for over 15 years and has served as an adjunct professor for Alamo Colleges teaching Dual Credit Government classes. She began her career teaching on-level World Geography, US History, Psychology, Sociology, and Economics. After spending a few years outside of education working in the private sector for a non-profit which provides mental health services, she returned to her true calling of teaching where she continues to teach, often simultaneously, AP Human Geography, AP World History, AP US History, AP US Government and Politics, AP Comparative Government, AP Macroeconomics, and AP Psychology. For the past several years, she has served as a celebrated grader of AP exams through CollegeBoard while she continues feeding her passion for teaching.

Kelsey Toms grew up in Los Angeles and attended Trinity University in San Antonio where she received a Bachelor of Arts in History and a Master of Arts in Teaching, specializing in Secondary Education. She has published peer-reviewed Understanding by Design (UbD) units on the Trinity University Digital Commons, including "AP United States History: Period 4 (1800-1848)," which utilizes the historical thinking skills and has been downloaded over 20,000 times. She has taught AP United States History, 8th and 11th grade US History, AP Psychology, and freshman Pre-AP Geography. She is now a Digital Coach at a middle school in Dallas, Texas helping teachers of all subjects leverage technology in the classroom through professional development and coaching.

Made in the USA
Las Vegas, NV
01 June 2023

72817637R00096